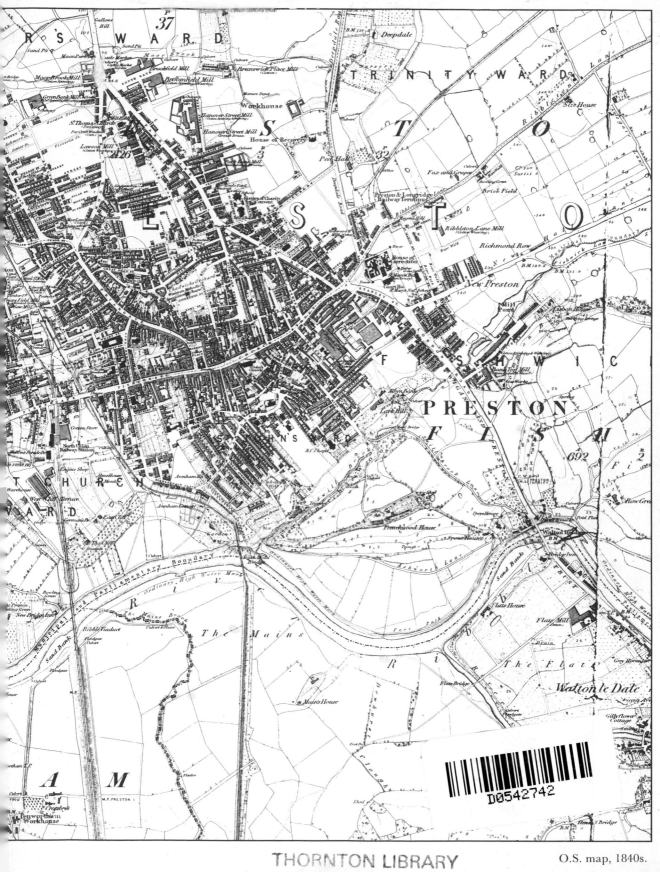

O.S. map, 1840s.

PRESTON
A Pictorial History

The obelisk in the Market Place, Preston, *c.*1840.

PRESTON
A Pictorial History

Geoffrey Timmins

Phillimore

1992

Published by
PHILLIMORE & CO. LTD.,
Shopwyke Hall, Chichester, Sussex

ISBN 0 85033 826 3

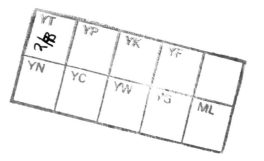

Printed and bound in Great Britain by
BIDDLES LTD.,
Guildford, Surrey

List of Illustrations

Frontispiece: The obelisk in the Market Place, *c.*1840

Acknowledgements

In preparing this book, I am particularly indebted to Ann Dennison and Terry Shaw of the Harris Reference Library and to Diana Winterbotham of Lancashire Local Studies Library, who between them unearthed most of the source material I required, including early maps. Terry, along with Nigel Morgan, Colin Stansfield and Colin Dickinson, read earlier drafts of the text and all suggested useful amendments or additions. Wally Rouse, company historian at British Aerospace Defence Limited, provided helpful information, whilst Bill Cowell gave invaluable assistance with photographic matters. My wife, Carol, helped in numerous ways and I thank her especially.

I gratefully acknowledge permission to reproduce the following illustrations: British Aerospace Defence Limited, 19a & b; Harris Museum and Art Gallery, 13b, 14a & b, 15c, 16c, 21c, 37b & c, 46b, 49b & c, 55b, 58a & b, 65, 67a, 74b, 75, 76, 79a, 81a, 85b; Harris Reference Library, 3, 6, 7, 9a, 10c, 13a, 15a, b & c, 16a & b, 17a & b, 18a, 20a, 23b, 26, 27c, 32, 38c, 41a & b, 43a & b, 44c, 49a, 51a & b, 52a & b, 54a & b, 55a, 56a & b, 57, 59b, 62b, 63a & b, 66a, 69a, 71, 73b, 77a & b, 78a, 80, 82, 84b, 86a & b, 87; *Lancashire Evening Post*, 17b, 18b, 20b, 34, 35, 56c, 61a, 62a, 72a & b, 81b, 84a & c, 88; Preston County Borough, 27a.

Introduction

If Lancashire towns were to be ranked according to their degree of visual attractiveness, Preston would certainly appear high on the list. Of course, non-Lancastrians might argue that this would say little, on the grounds that rival towns are hardly noted for their architectural splendours. A more informed response, though, would recognise that, despite some insensitive re-development, urban Lancashire has much to commend in terms of visual appeal and that Preston has far more to offer in this respect than is usual.

Such a view, however, is only sustainable with regard to the comparatively recent past. Indeed, before the late Georgian era, there were few buildings in any Lancashire town that had much architectural merit, a consequence of the limited wealth that the region had generated. It was not until the Victorian era that this situation altered dramatically. By then, the Lancashire economy was developing strongly, fuelled by a remarkable expansion of the cotton trade, which did not cease until the outbreak of the First World War.

At Preston, as elsewhere in urban Lancashire, economic growth during this period was associated with unprecedented increases in population size and in the extent of the built-up area. It also brought new opportunities to erect buildings of style and character. Such buildings reflect a flowering of civic pride and opulence and bear ample testimony to the town's growing importance.

Because the changes occurring in Preston during Victorian and Edwardian times were of such a fundamental nature, they are worthy of particular consideration. Accordingly, they provide the focus for this book. To concentrate on this era, however, is not to overlook the long-term perspective on Preston's development, for without it the full significance of the Victorian and Edwardian changes cannot be appreciated. The opening chapter, therefore, comprises a brief history of the town's evolution, charting its transition from an obscure manorial settlement in Norman times to a major urban centre in the 19th century. Twentieth-century developments are also outlined, considering how Preston's built environment has been adapted to meet the changing economic and social needs of its inhabitants.

The second chapter examines contemporary descriptions of Preston during the early years of Victoria's reign. These demonstrate the type of changes that were taking place, as well as offering contrasting interpretations of the quality of the town's built environment. They also provide a convenient base from which to analyse the main developments that occurred during ensuing decades.

The final chapter deals with these developments. Emphasis is placed on the physical expansion of the town, including the emergence of the earliest residential suburbs, the growth of factory industry and its associated housing, and the erection of religious and public buildings. In Preston, as elsewhere, it is these developments which have been largely responsible for creating the built environment and which, in large measure, still provide the town with its more distinctive characteristics.

1. Preston's Development: An Overview

The earliest documentary reference to Preston occurs in the Domesday Survey of 1086. Little detail is given, but there is enough to show that the settlement had gained some prominence as the chief manor of Amounderness (roughly the area of the modern Fylde). At the time of the Norman Conquest, no fewer than 61 local settlements belonged to it.[1] A church had also been built, the founding of which has been linked with Wilfrid, Abbot of Ripon. He is thought to have acquired land bordering the River Ribble and to have erected a church there during the early eighth century. At best, though, this theory remains tentative.[2]

There is nothing to suggest that Preston made any marked or sustained progress during the Anglo-Saxon era. At this time numerous boroughs were created for defensive and trading purposes, but none are known to have been in the area that eventually became Lancashire. This remained a remote and backward region, thinly populated and without monastic houses or towns.[3]

By Norman times, however, Preston had at least emerged as a centre of local importance, as the Domesday Survey shows. Its church, one of relatively few in the region,[4] provided a focal point for Christian gatherings and encouraged settlement. Moreover, Preston was well located, occupying a central position in the region and lying at the point where the main north/south through routes crossed the Ribble Valley. It also lay alongside a navigable estuary. Accordingly, it was always likely to attract visitors, traders especially.

To exploit these advantages, Preston's inhabitants needed freedom from manorial control. This they achieved through a series of royal charters, granted at intervals between the 12th and 19th centuries. Some of their earliest charter privileges are listed in a document known as the Preston Custumal, which probably dates from the early 14th century, but which could refer to a period up to two centuries before.[5]

Foremost amongst the early privileges was permission to form a guild merchant. This was an association of burgesses (townsmen and outsiders holding privileged position) which had power to regulate trade in the town. A membership fee was payable and members' names were entered on the guild roll. Non-guild members required leave to trade in the town and had to pay trading tolls, from which members, as freemen, were exempt. Additionally, the burgesses were allowed to hold a borough court or portmoot, which could deal with a wide range of offences including breaches of trading regulations. The portmoot also acted as governing body of the borough, eventually evolving into the town council, with its mayor, bailiffs (chief officers) and principal burgesses. In return for their privileges, the burgesses paid the monarch various rents and dues, known collectively as 'ferm'.

From time to time new charters were obtained, which confirmed the borough's privileges and extended their scope. For instance, that of 1227 allowed the burgesses to take timber from nearby Fulwood Forest for building purposes; that of 1252 to cultivate land on Preston Moor; and that of 1328 to hold a Wednesday market and an annual five-day fair in October.[6]

There is no evidence that, as was the case elsewhere, Preston's guild merchant became a permanent body. However, it did meet periodically to deal with such matters as collecting admittance and renewal dues, amending names on the guild roll and approving changes in trading regulations. The date of the earliest guild is uncertain, though it took place before 1328. From 1542 a guild has been held every 20 years.[7]

The privileges obtained by Preston's burgesses created a favourable environment for trade to develop, but trading rights could not guarantee economic success. Nor could they be easily maintained against manorial lords who were reluctant to lose their influence. Thus while 23 boroughs were founded in Lancashire between 1066 and 1372, only the four royal boroughs (Wigan, Preston, Lancaster and Liverpool) managed to retain their status as the Middle Ages closed.[8] Even for the successful towns setbacks occurred. Of particular note in Preston's case is the devastation perpetrated by the army of Robert the Bruce in 1322.[9]

Notwithstanding such disasters, Preston continued to expand during late medieval and early modern times. This is evident from the rising number of burgesses recorded on the guild rolls. That of 1397, the earliest available, names 325 from Preston (some of whom were sons of burgesses) and 33 outsiders. By 1582 the overall total had reached 1,000, up to two-thirds of whom were in-burgesses.[10] These figures hardly indicate rapid progress, but they do demonstrate that, by the Tudor period, Preston had developed into a trading centre of notable significance. Indeed, it was drawing trade from rival market centres such as Kirkham and Clitheroe.[11]

Contemporary visitors give some idea of the size and appearance of Tudor Preston. Writing c.1540, John Leland remarked that there was only one church and that the River Ribble 'goith round aboute a great Peace of the Grounde aboute Toune, yet it touchith not the Towne self by space of amost half a Mile'. Clearly the town occupied a highly confined site. Half a century later, William Camden reported that Preston was a 'large and, for these parts, handsome and populous towne ...'.[12] The qualification Camden makes is telling, serving as an apt reminder that towns in Lancashire were still small-scale and not especially attractive.

Nor was the situation appreciably different a century later, despite the economic advances made in Lancashire as textile production gathered pace. Using the hearth tax returns of 1662, it can be shown that no Lancashire town was amongst the first 40 in terms of total hearths taxed.[13] Furthermore, as in earlier times, severe checks on urban development occurred. These included a devastating outbreak of disease in the early 1630s, which may have killed over half of Preston's population and left only about nine hundred survivors.[14] The Civil War also exacted a dreadful toll on urban Lancashire, Preston being fortunate to escape its worst effects.[15]

Preston's population took a considerable time to recover from the 1631 crisis. Between 1717-19, baptisms recorded at the parish church averaged 113 per year, compared with 96 between 1676-9 and 143 between 1612-14.[16] Neither is it certain that the town's trading activity showed much expansion during these years. It is true that in-burgesses recorded on the guild rolls rose from around 800 in 1642 to 1,400 in 1682, but by this time, many lived elsewhere and were also registering their servants.[17] What growth occurred in Preston's population during the 17th century resulted partly from immigration. Guild orders sought to stem this, as it was felt too many immigrants were becoming 'chargeable to the town or troublesome by begging'. Measures taken included that of forbidding houses to be let to strangers, unless permission was obtained from the mayor and council.[18]

The guild records of this period also indicate the range and relative importance of Preston's trades, the 1642 guild roll noting the occupations of around 80 in-burgesses. They include 10 websters (weavers), eight shoemakers, seven husbandmen, seven taylors and five glovers. Altogether, 35 occupations are given.[19] Generalisations from such limited evidence are hazardous, although agriculture, along with trades based on animal products, still predominated. But a strong manufacturing sector led by linen and wool weaving had also emerged.

Other insights into Stuart Preston provided by the guild records concern public health, about which there was some anxiety. Apparently, 'refactory and ill-minded' inhabitants were neglecting to clean the street causeway in front of their houses and shops. Henceforth they were to do so every Saturday night. Dirt and dung was to be carried from the cause-way – its destination thereafter is not stipulated – whilst other refuse could be swept into the channel running along the centre of each street. There was also the problem of stray pigs, which trespassed into gardens and the churchyard, trampled corn and grass fields, and tore corn sacks on market days.[20] Control proved difficult to enforce, though, and led to such disquieting offences as 'keeping an unruly and unlawful sow', for which Henry Gregson's wife was summonsed in 1668.[21]

Despite these unsavoury revelations, contemporaries report that Preston was by this time acquiring a reputation as a genteel and stylish town, much frequented by those of social standing. For instance, Richard Kuerden, a local doctor and antiquary, remarked c.1684 that: 'This Borrough is much adorned with its large square, or market place, as likewise with the streets thereof, which are so spacious from one end thereof unto the other, that few of the Corporations of England exceed the same, either for streets or market-place'. He enthused also about the 'ample antient and yet well beautified Gylde or Town Hall' and the 'good handsome buildings' which were 'interwoven with stately fabricks of brickbuilding after the Modish manner'.[22]

Subsequent writers continued the theme. Ralph Thoresby of Leeds, in town for the 1702 guild, noted 'several very good houses',[23] whilst Daniel Defoe, a visitor in 1725, remarked that the town was 'full of attornies, proctors and notories' [1].[24] It was also the place to which those of social standing in Lancashire repaired during the winter. Included amongst them were the Stanleys, Earls of Derby, then the county's premier family.[25]

The presence of local gentry in Preston during the winter reflected the widespread practice amongst the leisured élite of spending the 'Season' (New Year to late spring) in London or some county town.[26] The attractions Preston offered in this respect included a mild climate and picturesque surroundings, as well as ease of access from all parts of the county, an important consideration when even the most wealthy had to endure the slowness and discomfort of horse-drawn travel [2]. Furthermore, with the financial backing of the town council, amenities aimed at a social élite were provided, including a racecourse at Preston Moor [10], a town hunt and, for more innocent pleasure, an elevated promenade at Avenham [3].[27] There was also the satisfaction to be derived from meeting with others of similar background and rank. Nor should it be overlooked that the local gentry visited Preston at other times of year, including when, in their capacity as county magistrates, they came to the Quarter Sessions and Special Sessions courts.[28] They were prominent, too, during guild celebrations, playing their full part in the colourful processions and being well represented at such exclusive events as the mayor's banquets.[29]

Throughout the 18th century, Preston retained its reputation as a town of quality, as efforts continued to extend its public amenities and enhance its appearance. They included a new bridge across the Ribble to Penwortham (1759) [4], an elegant assembly room provided by the Earl of Derby at the *Bull Inn* (*c*.1780) and additional places of worship, not least St Mary's Catholic chapel in Friargate (1761) and the Unitarian chapel in Percy Street (1716). There was rebuilding, too, including Patten House, home of the Stanleys in 1745, the Guild Hall in 1762 and the adjoining Town Hall in 1782 [5 & 6].[30]

During these years, Preston's economic functions remained varied. The traditional trades continued to be well represented; nearly all those recorded on the guild roll of 1642 still appeared in the trade directory lists of the early 19th century. The weekly markets, trading on Wednesdays, Fridays and Saturdays, were also maintained [7], as were the annual fairs, which took place in January, March and September, and the town retained its position as a major legal centre, with several borough and county courts holding regular sittings.[31]

By the end of the 18th century, however, Preston's economy was undergoing a profound transformation associated with technological advances in yarn spinning. These were greatly assisted by a Preston burgess, Richard Arkwright, whose water frame produced a cotton yarn sufficiently strong for use as a warp thread. Accordingly, an all-cotton cloth could be woven. Because Arkwright's machinery required a power source, it was used solely in factories. The other early spinning machines, Hargreaves' jenny and Crompton's mule, were also developed for factory use, the latter quickly growing to prominence.[32] Preston's first cotton spinning mill was opened at Moor Lane by Collinson and Watson in 1777 and the industry was greatly expanded by John Horrocks and his partners from the early 1790s [8].[33] By 1824, 16 cotton spinning firms were operating in the town.[34]

Textile weaving, meanwhile, remained largely unmechanised, production being organised on a domestic outwork basis. In Preston, as in other cotton towns, hand weavers became the most numerous occupational group, comprising about a quarter of all fathers listed in the town's Anglican baptism registers during the early 1820s. They formed a labour force of about four thousand people.[35] To meet their accommodation needs, 1,000 or more cottages were built, usually with cellar loomshops [9]. These constituted as much as a quarter of the town's total housing stock. Most were located on the north-west and south-east outskirts of the town, thereby contributing at an early stage to the major expansion of the built-up area that industrialisation was to bring [10].[36]

Preston's domestic outwork was partly organised by firms such as Horrocks, which both spun and wove, but there were also specialist manufacturers concentrating on weaving, 29 being listed in Baines' 1824 *Trade Directory*. Both types of employer probably utilised hand weavers in the surrounding rural areas, as well as those in town.

The rise of Preston's cotton industry was greatly facilitated by transport developments. The Lancaster canal, built in the early 1790s, had particular importance in providing an additional means of carrying coal to Preston, the only major textile town in Lancashire which lay distant from the coalfield [11]. Road improvements were also undertaken. In 1781 the bridge at Walton-le-Dale was replaced and during the mid-1820s Preston New Road was constructed, providing a third bridge across the Ribble and giving a much shorter and easier route to north-east Lancashire [12].[37] Improvements of this type were important in coping with the growing volume of commercial traffic, a good deal of which was generated by the domestic outwork system.

According to one strand of contemporary thought, the growth of the early cotton industry brought a fundamental change to the character of Preston. The view is neatly expressed by the journalist, Edward Baines. Writing in the mid-1820s, he urged that Preston, more than any other town in Lancashire, was characterised by persons of 'birth and polished manners'. During the preceding 40 years, however, this had changed, so that 'claims of gentility have been materially abated by the presence of an active and enterprising industry, which has served to place Preston more on a level than it formerly stood with the larger towns of the county'.[38] Had Baines been reviewing his observation later in the century, he might have concluded that this process of social levelling had gone even further. At any rate, Preston continued to develop strongly as an industrial town, with cotton production well to the fore. During the middle decades of the century, cotton weaving was absorbed into the factory system and power weavers emerged as by far the biggest element in Preston's labour force. By 1911, they numbered an astonishing 18,000, comprising one third the overall total, and half that for females [13]. At the same time, the textile trades as a whole employed over 28,000 people, about half the town's workforce, whilst the number of cotton mill premises in the town exceeded sixty.[39]

Other manufacturing activity also developed in Preston during the 19th century, metal working and engineering being the most important. These trades embraced a wide range of activity, including the manufacture of textile and printing machinery, tramcars and marine engineering products [14]. Collectively, they employed some 5,000 men in 1911, about 14 per cent of the male labour force. Transport absorbed a similar proportion of males, railways and roads [15] employing far more than the docks, which, amidst controversy about the cost involved, had been erected during the early 1890s [16].[40] As far as females were concerned, the biggest employment opportunity outside textiles was in domestic service.

Preston's emergence as a major textile centre was accompanied by an unprecedented increase in its physical size, an issue considered in subsequent chapters. It also saw a rapid rise in population, migration into the town and high birth rates, proving more than sufficient to counteract appallingly high mortality levels.[41] The result was a doubling of population during the Victorian and Edwardian era, reaching 117,088 by 1911, thereby ensuring that Preston remained amongst Lancashire's most populous towns.[42]

Cotton textile production continued to expand in Lancashire until World War One [17]. The war years, however, brought disruption to overseas markets and recovery during the post-war decades was hindered by increased overseas competition and lack of investment in new technology.[43] Surplus capacity became a growing problem in the industry, and at Preston, as elsewhere, machinery was scrapped and mills closed. By the early 1990s, only two Preston firms were still engaged in textile spinning and weaving.[44]

As cotton declined, replacement industry developed relatively quickly, aided by the town's excellent communications [18].[45] Some was in manufacturing, including rayon making, started at Courtaulds Red Scar works in the late 1930s, and aircraft production, to which the English Electric Company turned in the late 1930s [19].[46] Increasing reliance, though, has been placed on service industries. By 1987, fewer than 20 per cent of Preston's workforce was employed in manufacturing, compared with 75 per cent in services.[47] In part the service occupations reflect the town's traditional trading and legal functions, despite the docks being closed in 1981. But Preston has also been the administrative centre for Lancashire County Council since its inception in 1889.[48] In more recent years, too, it has become a major centre of higher education, Preston (later Lancashire) Polytechnic being designated in 1973 [20].[49]

Accompanying the change in economic function has been a partial redevelopment of the town centre. This has largely taken place since the 1960s, its legacy including several multi-storey office blocks, as dominant as they are undistinguished; a replacement bus station, surmounted by a tiered car park with its remarkable overhanging floors [21]; and, in Lancaster Road, a new Guild Hall [22], the scale and style of which contrasts so markedly with the range of classical revival buildings opposite, that it has been likened to 'a colossal lunar landing craft which has lost its way'.[50] The inevitable shopping malls have appeared as well, St George's dating from the mid-1960s (but refurbished a decade later) [23] and the Fishergate Centre [24] from the late 1980s.

There has also been substantial housing redevelopment. During the inter-war years the first council estates were erected on the town outskirts at Ribbleton, Deepdale and Ashton [25]. Between 1921 and 1936, 2,625 council houses were built in Preston, compared with 3,535 by private firms.[51] Yet housing problems remained acute, a survey in 1951 estimating that no fewer than 15,000 new houses were needed to replace unfit dwellings and relieve overcrowding [26].[52] Much of this unfit housing was dealt with between the mid-1950s and late 1960s, when massive clearance programmes brought the demolition of over 7,500 inner-area dwellings, mainly in the Avenham and Adelphi districts [27].[53] Redevelopment in both places included high-rise blocks [28]. With 11.2 per cent of Preston's housing still regarded as unfit in 1973, further substantial clearances took place.[54] Replacement housing spilled out into the surrounding rural areas, the population of which rose by about 25 per cent between 1971 and 1981.[55] Meanwhile the growing fashion for refurbishing older property led to the designation of improvement areas, as at Plungington [29]. In recent years, however, public expenditure controls have curbed both clearance and rebuilding programmes [30].[56]

The changes taking place in Preston during the last few decades have transformed the appearance of the town. The dominant forest of mill chimneys, interspersed with ornate church spires, has given way to high-rise housing and office blocks, starkly functional and highly pervasive [31]. Now, as in the past, not all new intrusions on Preston's townscape are unreservedly welcome.

References
1. D. W. Clemesha, *A History of Preston in Amounderness* (1912), pp.7-8.
2. E. Baines, *History, Directory and Gazetteer of the County Palatine of Lancaster* (1825), II, p.473.
3. J. J. Bagley, *A History of Lancashire* (1976), pp.27-28, 43.
4. Ibid., p.24. Around 25 churches were to be found.
5. On the date of the Custumal and the privileges conferred by Preston's early charters, see W. A. Abram, *Memorials of the Preston Guild* (1882), p.6; Clemesha, *op. cit.*, pp.41-57; S. Sartin, *Historic Preston* (1988); A. Crosby, *The History of Preston Guild* (1990), pp.4-14.
6. Abram, *op. cit.*, pp.3-4.
7. For a discussion, see Clemesha, *op. cit.*, ch.4; and Crosby, *op. cit.*, pp.15-17.
8. R. Millward, *Lancashire: an Illustrated Essay on the History of the Landscape* (1955), p.68.
9. Baines, *op. cit.*, p.475.
10. Abram, *op. cit.*, pp.10, 13.
11. T. W. Freeman, H. B. Rodgers and R. H. Kinvig, *Lancashire, Cheshire and the Isle of Man* (1966), p.49.
12. Both are quoted in Baines, *op. cit.*, p.476.
13. W. G. Hoskins, *Local History in England* (1959), p.177.
14. Clemesha, *op. cit.*, pp.118-20.
15. A. C. Hodge, *History of Preston* (1984), p.13.
16. Lancashire Record Office, *Preston Parish Registers* (microfilm copy).

17. Abram, *op. cit.*, pp.47-48; Crosby, *op. cit.*, pp.47-48.
18. W. Dobson and J. Harland, *A History of Preston Guild* (1862), p.44.
19. W. A. Abram, *The Rolls of Burgesses at the Guilds Merchant of the Borough of Preston* (1884), pp.94-105. These figures refer only to the initial list of some 800 in-burgesses.
20. W. A. Abram, *Memorials of the Preston Guilds* (1882), p.54.
21. Dobson and Harland, *op. cit.*, p.41.
22. A. Hewitson, *History of Preston* (1887), pp.35-37.
23. Abram, *op. cit.*, p.74.
24. D. Defoe, *A Tour Through the Whole Island of Great Britain* (1986 reprint of 1724-26 edition), p.548.
25. Clemesha, *op. cit.*, p.171. Above all else, perhaps, this gave Preston its unofficial position as Lancashire's county town, a status actually accorded to Lancaster. For a discussion of county towns in the 18th century, see P. Borsay, *The Eighteenth Century Town: A Reader in English Urban History* (1990), ch.3.
26. See, for example, H. Perkin, *The Railway Age* (1971), ch.8.
27. J. Walton, *Lancashire: A Social History, 1558-1939* (1987), pp.80-81; Borsay, *op. cit.*, pp.161-62.
28. Clemesha, *op. cit.*, pp.156-60.
29. See, for example, Abram, *op. cit.*, pp.92-93.
30. Clemesha, *op. cit.*, pp.315, 323; Sartin, *op. cit.*, p.47.
31. J. Aiken, *A Description of the Country from Thirty to Forty Miles Around Manchester* (1795), pp.284-86. For guild roll occupational data in the 18th century, see Borsay, *op. cit.*, pp.164-67 and 182-87.
32. A. E. Musson, *The Growth of British Industry* (1978), pp.81-82.
33. Clemesha, *op. cit.*, p.215.
34. Baines, *op. cit.*, p.513.
35. J. G. Timmins, *The Decline of Handloom Weaving in Nineteenth Century Lancashire*, unpublished PhD thesis, Lancaster University (1990), p.72.
36. For a fascinating discussion, see N. Morgan, *Vanished Dwellings* (1990).
37. Timmins, *op. cit.*, p.107.
38. Baines, *op. cit.*, p.504.
39. The occupational details are from the 1911 Census Report, *Occupations and Industries*, Vol.X, II (1913), pp.236-38 and the cotton firm numbers from P. Barrett & Co., *General and Commercial Directory of Preston* (1913), pp.332-33.
40. See especially J. Barron, *A History of the Ribble Navigation* (1938), ch.VI.
41. In 1851, about half Preston's population were migrants. (M. Anderson, *Family Structure in Nineteenth Century Lancashire* (1971), p.203.)
42. 1911 Census Report, X, II, p.236.
43. Walton, *op. cit.*, pp.325-33.
44. *Preston Business Directory* (1991), p.95.
45. Freeman et al., *op. cit.*, p.223-24.
46. *Preston and District Official and Industrial Handbook* (*c*.1969), p.102.
47. *Preston Business Directory* (1991), p.5.
48. J. D. Marshall (ed.), *The History of Lancashire County Council* (1977), pp.3-4, 53-54.
49. G. Timmins, D. Foster and H. Law, *Preston Polytechnic: the Emergence of an Institution, 1828-1978* (1979), p.42.
50. Sartin, *op. cit.*, p.19.
51. County Borough of Preston, *Report of Medical Officer of Health* (1936), p.44.
52. *Development Plan for the County Borough of Preston* (1951), p.20.
53. County Borough and Port of Preston, *Report on the Health of the Borough* (1969), p.81.
54. North West Joint Planning Team, *Strategic Plan for the North West* (1974), p.110.
55. Preston Borough Council, *Preston Rural Areas Local Plan, 1987-1997* (1987), p.10. The figures refer to rural areas north of the Ribble.
56. Lancashire County Council, *Structure Plan: Explanatory Memorandum* (1967), p.22.

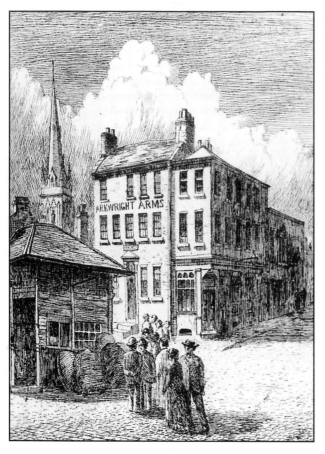

1. Amongst the high-quality dwellings to be found in Preston during the early 18th century were Arkwright House, in Stonygate, where Richard Arkwright was to develop his cotton spinning machinery, and the house in Church Street, which was to become the town's first bank. Both were provided with three storeys, the former having a pedimented doorway and the latter a two-storeyed porch surmounted by a balustrade. Arkwright House survives, though it has been extensively modernised.

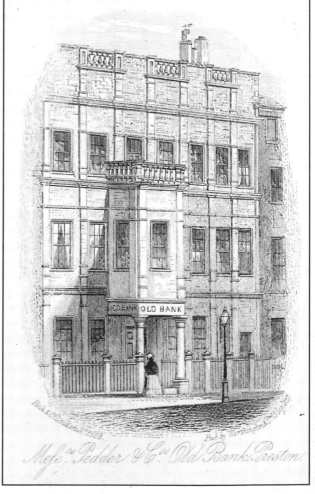

Mess.rs Pedder & Co. Old Bank, Preston.

2. This map extract is from Aiken's *Description of the Country ... Around Manchester*, published in 1795. Roads are recorded rather selectively and the route of the Leeds-Liverpool Canal through north-east Lancashire is projected rather than actual. Even so, the map clearly demonstrates Preston's emergence as a major route centre, accessible both by sea and canal and having direct road links to Manchester and Liverpool.

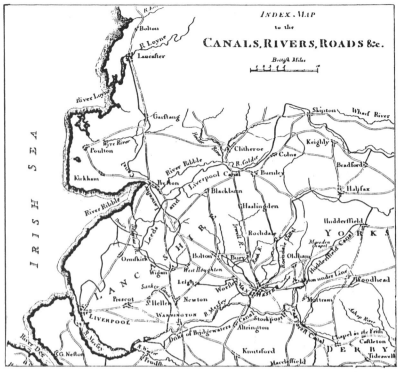

3. This extract from the engraving made by S. and N. Buck in 1728 shows the prominence of the tree-lined Avenham Walks (no. 8) and indicates the type of unrestricted views that could be obtained of the surrounding countryside. Several high-quality houses are shown, including Patten House (no. 9) which was occupied by the Earl of Derby. To the west of the parish church, along Fishergate, are a number of houses with long, narrow gardens. These originated as burgage plots (land held by privileged townsmen and outsiders known as burgesses). Others were to be found off Church Street and Friargate. They were gradually infilled during the 18th and 19th centuries, often with crowded, insanitary housing.

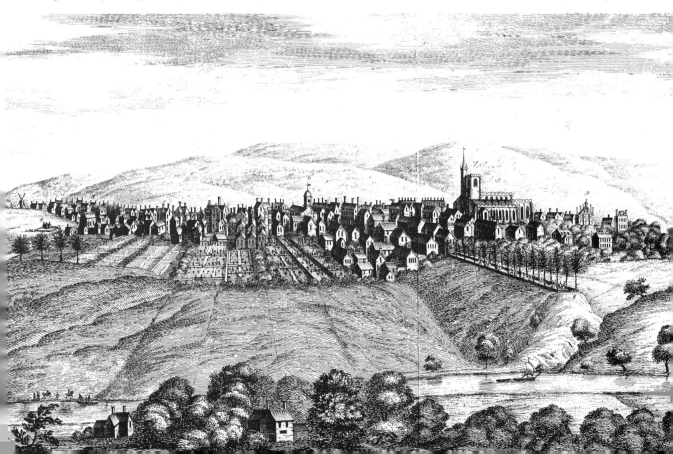

4. Before the mid-18th century, access from Penwortham to Preston involved fording the Ribble. This was generally hazardous and could prove fatal (see Hardwick, *History of the Borough of Preston*, 1857, pp.459-60). The ford was downstream of the bridge so that on each side of the river the established route had to be diverted upstream, as Yates' map [10] reveals. This, combined with its steepness and narrowness, made the bridge less than convenient. However, it was not until 1912 that a wider and flatter replacement bridge was built.

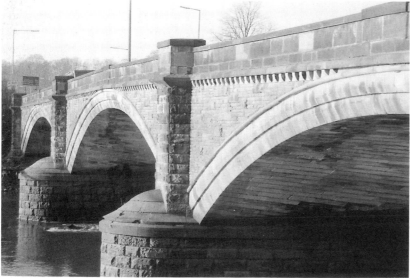

5. Classical in style, the Guild Hall had a symmetrical frontage with rusticated stonework at ground-floor level and brick above. Decoration was concentrated on the central bays, arched windows being provided at first-floor level and a pediment at the top. The Town Hall was of similar style. Its tower featured corner pilasters and louvred bell openings and was surmounted by a cupola, with four clock-faces and a weather vane. A chiming public clock had particular value at a time when relatively few individuals owned clocks or watches.

6. Between 1770 and 1817, rebuilding also took place at the parish church, a revived decorated style being preferred, as this 1820s engraving of Church Street reveals. The new tower, erected in 1814, added some architectural interest to an otherwise undistinguished street.

7. This illustration of the Market Place, dating from around the start of Victoria's reign, shows a group of female traders clustered around the steps of the familiar obelisk, which was then gas-lit. The clock tower of the Town Hall is visible. On the south side of the square is a group of four-storeyed, timber-framed buildings, with jetties and gables, the ground-floor rooms of which were then used as shops.

8. Horrocks' first premises, the Yellow Factory, was modest enough in terms of scale and style, as the first illustration (drawn *c*.1880) reveals. The Yard Works, however, of which it formed a part, had grown appreciably by the mid-19th century, boasting several large, functional blocks of six storeys or more. By this time, other substantial cotton firms had emerged in the town, including Swainson and Birley, which erected its massive Fishwick Mills off London Road in 1823.

Mess.rs Horrocks, Miller & Co.s Yard Factory, Preston.

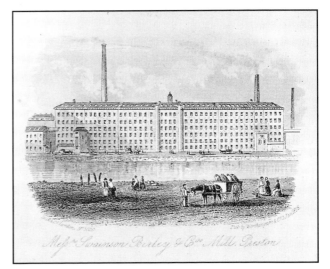

Mess.rs Swainson Birley & Co.s Mills, Preston.

9. Cellar loomshops provided the damp conditions necessary for weaving cotton. These examples, probably photographed in the inter-war years, were in Mount Pleasant. off Friargate. The cellars protruded above ground level to improve natural lighting, although this brought the inconvenience of steps to the front and rear doors. Many such cottages, recognisable by these steps, can be seen on the five feet to the mile O.S. map of the 1840s. The extract shows examples in Heatley Street, also off Friargate.

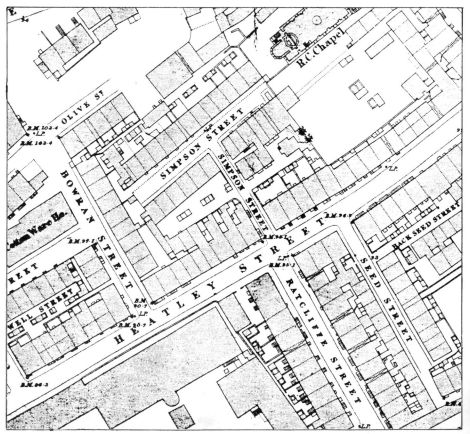

10. Comparison of Yates' map (1786) with that of Greenwood (1818) reveals appreciable expansion, most noticeably to the north-west of the town centre, between Friargate and the canal, and to the east between Church Street and London Road. The Yates extract also shows the Moor Park racecourse, used until 1791. Later races were held on Fulwood Moor and at Penwortham Holme, originally an island in the Ribble. The engraving shows those held at the Holme to celebrate the 1842 Guild. (For details of political rivalry associated with horse racing in Preston, see A. Hewitson, *A History of Preston*, 1883, p.120.)

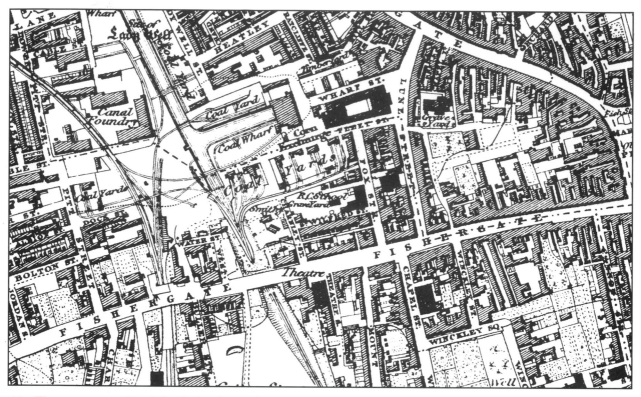

11.   The numerous coal yards bordering the canal to the north of Fishergate bear testimony to the immense amount of coal brought into Preston by both canal and railway. The extract is from the six inch to the mile O.S. map of the early 1840s. Coal arriving by canal crossed the Ribble Valley on a tramway which passed under Fishergate, close to the theatre. According to one contemporary critic, the tramway was erected in 'an evil hour, instead of an aqueduct ...'. Barges were hauled up the slope at Avenham by steam engine. The tramway bridge and the steam engine chimney stack can both be seen in the illustration from the 1850s.

12.   The steep sides of the Ribble Valley brought problems for road builders seeking to provide gentle slopes for horse-drawn traffic. Their main solution was to make cuttings in the upper reaches of the valley sides. The example shown is on Penwortham Brow, to the south of Preston, the road crossing the Ribble by means of the old bridge at Penwortham. The engraving dates from 1842.

13. Female weavers predominate in the above photograph taken at Horrocks' Centenary Mill *c*.1920. As was generally the case, they were in the younger age groups, as married women tended to cease work once they had families. In 1911, nearly 80 per cent of Preston's female weavers were under the age of 35 and above half were under twenty-five. Spinning, by contrast, was male-orientated. Characteristically, the mule spinner in the photograph below, who may also have been employed by the Horrocks' concern *c*.1920, found footwear uncomfortable and preferred to work in bare feet.

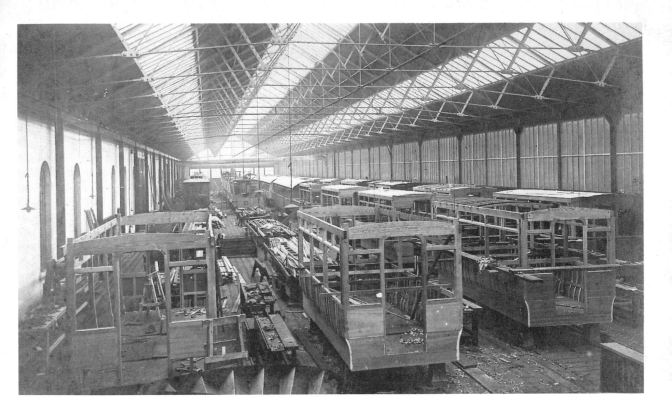

14. Tramcar production in Preston was associated with Dick, Kerr and Company, at whose works in Strand Road these photographs were taken in the early 1900s.

15. The cart driver photographed at Horrocks' works serves as a reminder that much of Preston's road transport in the early 20th century remained unmechanised. Accordingly, numerous stables were still required, that shown in the photograph overleaf accommodating horses owned by the town council. Long-haul traffic, meanwhile, was largely handled by rail, which, as the photographs taken at Preston station reveal, assumed a new, though disturbing, significance during the First World War.

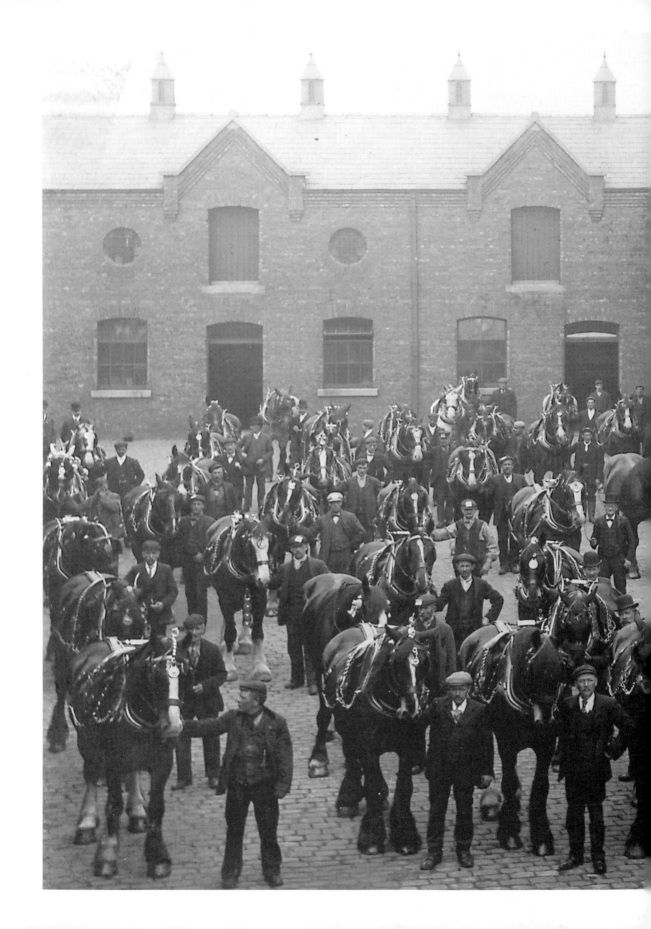

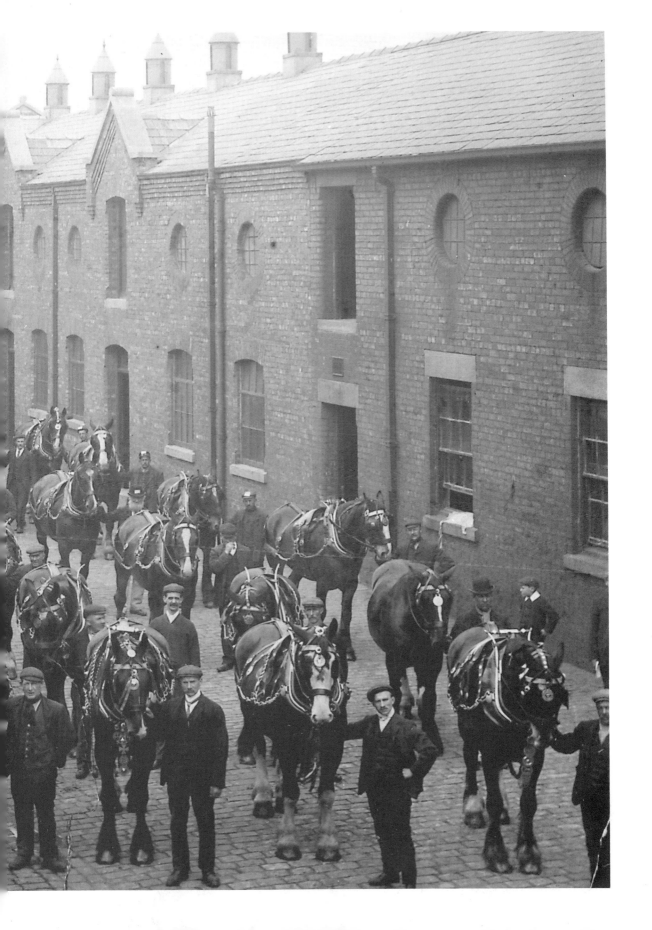

16.   Timber formed one of the principal imports handled at the docks; a handbook of 1920 refers to some 80,000 tons being landed annually. Livestock imports were considerable too, the docks being equipped with extensive lairage facilities. Amongst exports, coal was to the fore. The photograph shows a coal wagon lift, which enabled coal to be loaded on to ships by means of a chute.

17. The elevated photograph, taken in the mid-1930s, gives a view north-west along Friargate. It demonstrates the extent to which the townscape of Preston's industrial zone was characterised by factory chimneys when the textile trade was still a major industry. Along with the Fishergate photograph opposite, it also demonstrates how the central part of the town was dominated by commercial functions. Most evident are the three-storey shop premises, usually with elaborate frontages, which bordered the main streets.

18. Preston's communications were substantially improved in 1912 by the construction of an additional bridge across the Ribble to Penwortham. The photographs, probably dating from the inter-war years, show a much flatter and wider structure than that of the earlier bridge.

19. The English Electric Company, which had made a small number of aircraft in the 1920s, turned to the production of Halifax and Hampden bombers during the Second World War. Almost 3,000 were produced at their Strand Road Works. These photographs show front sections of Halifax bombers and workers in the inspection department.

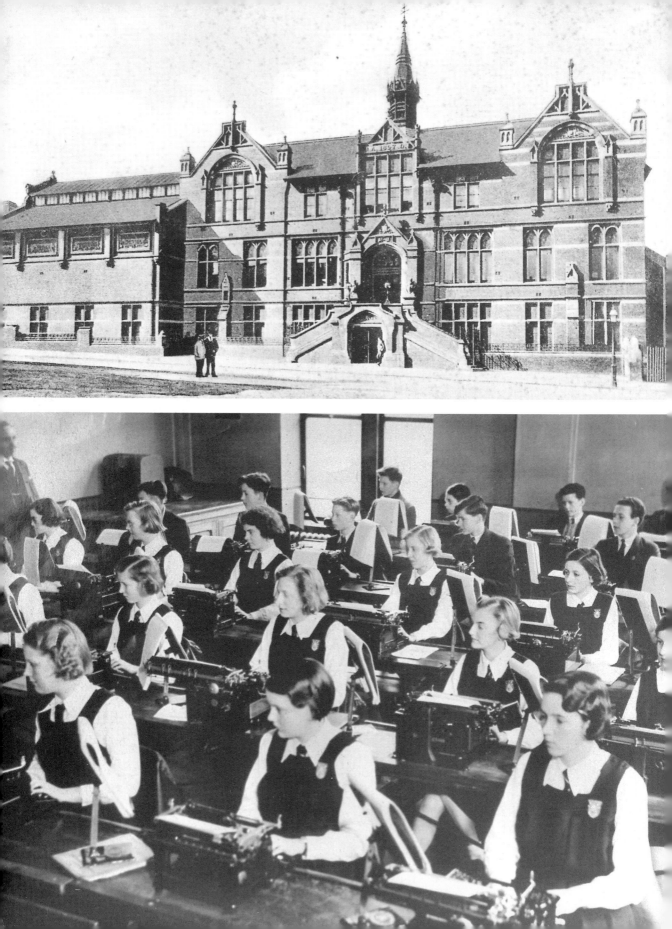

20. Following a bequest under the will of E. R. Harris, a local solicitor, the Institution for the Diffusion of Knowledge changed its name to the Harris Institute, and in 1897 the Victoria Jubilee Technical School was opened. Situated in Corporation Street, the building has a symmetrical, Tudor-style façade, as the early 20th-century photograph reveals, and was substantially extended in 1931. Junior commercial and technical classes were established, the photograph of pupils attending the former being taken in 1939. The building now comprises the Harris Building of Lancashire Polytechnic.

21. The extraordinary length of the tiered car-park adds a strongly horizontal dimension to this part of the Preston townscape, providing a welcome change from the vertical dominance of the surrounding office blocks. The older photograph is of the rather cramped and undistinguished bus station which formerly occupied the site. It was demolished in the late 1960s.

22.   Opened in the guild year of 1972, the Guild Hall is a striking example of a building inspired by the modern movement in architecture. Thus, there is little concern to hide its structural features, the first-floor perimeter being open-sided, revealing pillars and cross-beams which support the enclosed upper storey. Reinforced concrete and brick prevail, and decoration is avoided.

23. The exterior photographs are of the Fishergate entrance to St George's Centre and the façade of the former gas company office and showrooms it replaced. The newer edifice scarcely adds architectural interest to the street, a charge which cannot be made of its Gothic-style predecessor. The interior photograph shows the central display area from which three shopping arcades radiate. It was taken in the early 1980s following refurbishment, which included roofing over the central area. Professor Pevsner declares the original concept to be good, but the details 'a bit garish'.

24. The façade of Fishergate Centre returns to a more decorative building style. Arcading on the frontage is emphasised by the use of light-coloured brickwork, a feature of the interior walls also, whilst the entrance is formed by terminating the shopping arcade roof in a high, round-arched canopy of steel and glass. Pevsner would probably have found the interior detail more restrained than that in St George's Centre, though the extensive use of roof claddings with polished surfaces may be regarded as rather showy.

25. Early council housing in Preston follows a more general trend in design, strongly influenced by the garden city movement. Instead of the traditional grid-iron terraces, semi-detached houses and short terraces were preferred, each set in its own garden and approached, in many instances, along curvilinear streets. They were designed for upper working- and lower middle-class families. (See M. Savage, *The Dynamics of Working-Class Politics*, 1987, p.116.) These examples are off London Road.

26. This photograph of Nile Street, off Church Street, was taken in the 1950s and shows a typical example of the type of housing considered to be unfit. The shop and public houses serve as a reminder that a major drawback of large-scale redevelopment was the disruption it brought to established community life.

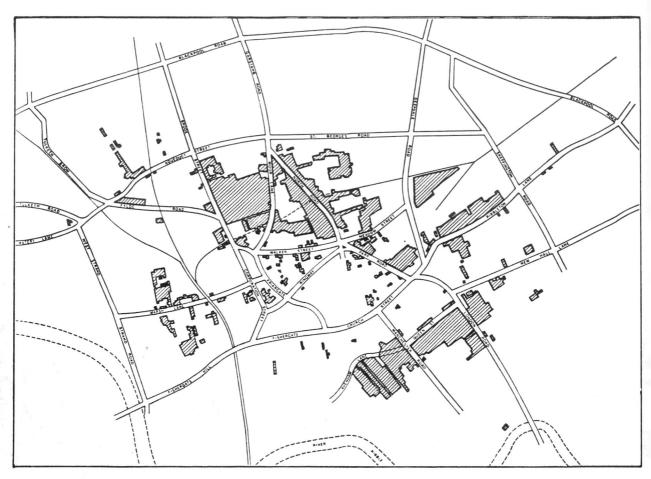

27.   The map records the extent of demolition that took place in Preston during the 1950s and '60s, whilst the photograph of redevelopment at Avenham records a scene that became all too familiar in the town at this time. Demolition also brought a fundamental alteration to the town's industrial landscape, especially with the dismantling of mill chimneys. The photograph shows one of the last to survive, that at Stocks Bridge Mill, Eldon Street, which was taken down in January 1992.

28. A tenants' handbook of 1950 reveals Preston Council was uneasy about erecting high-rise flats. However, only four disadvantages were listed compared with 12 advantages. The latter included privacy and ease of cleaning. Most redevelopment, though, has been low-rise and varying designs have been adopted. They include three- and four-storeyed terraces at Avenham, fitted with heavy, arched lintels made from concrete, and factory-built housing of timber-framed construction, erected off Lancaster Road. Both types date from the 1960s.

29. As elsewhere, improvements to Victorian terraces have become widespread in Preston. They include path and road resurfacing, provision of parking spaces, tree and shrub planting, and designation of one-way streets. This example is in Plungington.

30. The other major redevelopment has been at the dockland site, where new leisure and shopping facilities have been provided, as well as housing. The view in this picture, taken from the marina during the summer of 1991, looks eastwards towards the town.

31. Comparison of the mid-19th century engravings with the modern photograph demonstrates clearly how Preston's townscape has changed to reflect a service rather than a manufacturing function. Even so, glimpses of an earlier townscape are still to be found, as at the junction of Stanley Street and New Hall Lane. Prominent are Centenary Mill (1895 with 1850s chimney), St Mary's church (1838), the prison governor's house (1834), and, in the right foreground, the former court house (1825).

2. Early Victorian Preston

The Progressive View

On visiting Preston in 1836, Sir George Head, retired military commissar turned popular writer, was greatly impressed by developments on the town's outskirts at Avenham. In the account of his visit he remarks: 'Amongst the suburbs of the southern extremity, where ample space has been allotted to the streets and houses, many of which, of a superior description, have been erected within a few years, the eye is refreshed by handsome elevations of bright red brick, embellished by healthy young trees' [32]. He enthuses, too, about the views obtainable from the raised promenade at Avenham Walks [33]: 'The prospect below extends over a charming valley, wherein the River Ribble meanders through a country rich in groves, pastures, and stately timber, and further ornamented by gentlemen's seats and white farmhouses, which latter are scattered among the green fields in considerable profusion'. So profoundly was he moved by the charm of his surroundings, that he could not refrain from romantic excess:

> It was on a summer's evening at the approach of night that I visited this spot, when the gas-lights, one after another, started into existence, reflected an emerald lustre from the green leaves, bearing the hue of glow-worms in the shade, and so vivid, as to raise before the fancy the picture of an illuminated garden.[1]

Other contemporary accounts refer with equal approval to the manner in which Preston was developing. They include that in Mannex's 1851 *Trade Directory*. In common with Head, the author found much to commend at Avenham, not least the newly-opened Avenham Institute [34 & 35]. This was the home of the Preston Institution for the Diffusion of Knowledge, a body which sought to educate operative mechanics. Built in a Grecian style, the institute was 'one of the most elegant structures in the town ...', occupying a 'delightful situation' near the entrance to Avenham Walks [36]. Surprisingly, the Mannex writer does not comment on the growing number of desirable, middle-class houses bordering the nearby Winckley Square [37]. Yet he does mention the 'splendid range of Tudor-style buildings' situated at the junction of Winckley Square and Cross Street. Built during the 1840s, they housed the Literary and Philosophical Institution, a long-established competitor of the Institution for the Diffusion of Knowledge; the exclusive Winckley Club, with its news and billiard rooms; and the Grammar School [38], which gave fee-paying boys a classical education.[2]

One middle-class housing development that does receive attention is the 'magnificent Grecian terrace' situated along Deepdale Road on the eastern outskirts of the town. Known as Stephenson Terrace, it was built in 1849-50 [39]:

> The whole at first sight has a picturesque appearance, and presents to the beholder 'uniformity and elegance combined'. The vestibule to the front of each building is embellished with two columns and parapets, and the gardens, pallisading, and gateways, give them the appearance of the villas at Venice.[3]

Also singled out for their architectural attractions are the Corn Exchange and Market House, 'a handsome brick structure' in Lune Street [40 & 41] and the Guild Hall and Town Hall, 'a stately pile' by the market place [5].[4] In fact, even those most functional of buildings, the barracks at Fulwood and the house of correction in Stanley Street, were thought to have visual merit. At the former, the 'neat chapel' was seen to add architectural character to a 'large mass of substantial building' [42 & 43].[5] At the latter, the eye was caught by the governor's house, a 'handsome castellated building', strikingly decorated with the arms of the Duchy of Lancaster [44].[6]

Amongst other buildings in Preston to impress early Victorian commentators were the various churches and chapels, of which, in 1841, there were eight belonging to the Anglicans, four to Catholics and 13 to the Nonconformists.[7] Mostly erected during the two previous decades, they were accorded glowing appreciation. Thus, in 1837 Peter Whittle, one of Preston's early historians, enthused about St Peter's church [45]: 'It is a very chaste and beautiful specimen of Gothic Architecture ... There is a handsome stained window done by Mr. Seaward of Lancaster, which overlooks the altar. The whole is beautifully ornamented with the arms of Preston, and other gentlemen of the town'.[8]

As well as extolling the visual enhancement of Preston's townscape, early Victorians highlight progress in other aspects of the town's development. With regard to public utilities, for example, they note eagerly that Preston was the first provincial town to install gas lighting. This was as early as 1816, and by mid-century no fewer than 1,000 public gas lamps were in use.[9]

Preston's other public utility, the waterworks, also draws praiseworthy comment. An Act of Parliament secured in 1832 enabled the town's first reservoirs to be built, bringing the expectation of an abundant supply of pure water. It is confidently reported that a good mains pressure was obtained, a trial undertaken in Lune Street demonstrating that a hosepipe could be discharged over houses three storeys in height.[10]

As to industrial development, statistics portraying rapid advance are proudly announced. For instance, it is noted that there were 35 cotton mills in the town in 1838, compared with 16 in 1819 and only about six in 1802.[11] The impact they had on the formation of industrial colonies is carefully charted. Thus, in 1837, Whittle could report: 'At the west end of the town, and on each side of Marsh-lane ... which was but lately through fields and gardens, several new cotton and linen mills present themselves ... and the street consisting of artizans dwellings is fast extending towards the River Ribble'. He notes similar trends on the northern and eastern outskirts, including a 'very extensive' addition at the Horrocks' Yard Works.[12]

Amongst further developments that excited Preston's early Victorians were transport improvements. In the case of railways, Mannex's 1851 directory lists no fewer than seven lines which had converged on Preston during the preceding 12 years. The impressive dimensions of the bridges and viaducts built to accommodate these lines are closely detailed [46]. That Preston had become such a significant railway centre led one mid-century writer to comment, no doubt with substance, that the town's Fishergate station was amongst the busiest in the country.[13] It was also seen as a visual asset, being described as 'an elegant Grecian building of stone' [47].[14]

Also busy was the quay, where once again recent improvements could be highlighted. By Act of Parliament passed in 1838, the Ribble Navigation Company built new bonded warehouses on the quay and deepened the Ribble estuary by some six feet [48]. As a result, vessels of 200 tons capacity could reach the quay with the aid of spring tides. In 1849 the ports of Preston and Fleetwood accepted 1,721 coasting vessels, as well as 59 from overseas. Of these, 574 coasting vessels came to Preston, along with 23 from abroad.[15]

No contemporary record of Preston's early Victorian improvements could ignore the provision of public parkland and the council received high praise for creating Moor Park during the late 1830s [49]:

> To crown the whole, the corporation have set a rare and powerful example, by laying out Preston Moor, and intersecting it with magnificent walks, etc., for promenading, which will be of use as to public health and recreation.
> This is a most important undertaking, and ... for invalids it will be most desirable and salubrious, all classes are free here, as it is offered without restraint by the munificences of the corporation.[16]

To comment on environmental enhancement of this type could be added that of Preston's natural advantages of site. These included adequate space to permit the developments which so thrilled contemporaries, an advantage which Peter Whittle forecast could have the most far-reaching consequences:

> The town is in fact, creeping out in numerous directions, and it is gratifying to remark, that the elevated, airy, and delightful site upon which Preston stands ... affords ample room, within boundaries conveniently marked out by nature, for its compact extension to the magnitude of a city of the first class.[17]

The Discordant View

Whilst some contemporary writings offer a very positive image of early Victorian Preston, others provide a perspective which is altogether less wholesome and far more worthy of condemnation than of praise. Its main characteristics are graphically recorded in a sanitary report on the town prepared by the Rev. John Clay in 1844. He summarises them as:

> defective ventilation, cleansing and draining of streets; the same evils with regard to dwellings; the over-crowding of rooms and of beds; filthiness of apartments, persons, clothing and bedding; prevalence of damp, yet want of water; absence of proper and decent accommodation as to privies; keeping of pigs in, or too near, dwellings; and, pervading all, sickening smells ...[18]

He also mentions smoke pollution, which was most acute on the north-east side of the town, in the path of the prevailing south-westerlies. Land here was used for market gardening, and although the smoke did not prevent vegetables from growing, additional labour was required to remove the soot falling on them.[19]

In considering examples of inadequate sanitation, Clay highlights the conditions he found at Back Queen Street, which bordered Horrocks' Yard Works on the south-east edge of the town [50]. It was approached by several lobbies (narrow passages) running through the terraced houses in Queen Street:

> A visitor, on entering the former, finds himself facing a row of privies of more than 100 yards long. The doors of the privies are about six feet from the house doors opposite; and the space between one privy and another is filled up with all imaginable and unimaginable filth; so that the street consists of a passage a little more than six feet wide, with dwelling houses on one side, and a continuous range of necessaries, pigsties, middens, heaps of ashes, etc., etc., on the other, with a filthy and sluggish surface drain running along one side.

Clay does not describe conditions inside these houses, but he does for dwellings elsewhere in the town. He quotes, for example, the case of a night watchman who lodged in a low room less than seven feet by five feet, which was lit by a roof light only nine inches square. He shared the room with 'an old man labouring under paralysis'. More disturbing was the case of the shoemaker who lived in a room with his wife and three children. Under the room he kept a pig: 'A sow belonging to a friend, having brought forth a more numerous litter than she could support, the shoemaker fitted up, for the reception of the supernumerary pigs, a corner of his living room ...'.[20]

As was usual with compilers of Victorian sanitary reports, Clay relies almost exclusively on written descriptions. However, he does include a drawing and plan of two rows of cottages separated at the rear by a narrow passage [51].[21] He explains that the passage functioned as a cesspool, receiving 'the Contents of the Privies & Drains, & the Ashes and refuse of the whole Block'. The resulting accumulations were removed no more than twice a year and then only to be deposited in heaps nearby [52].

Another report on Preston's sanitation, prepared in 1849 by George Thomas Clark, Superintending Inspector of the General Board of Health, provides equally disgusting instances of insanitary streets and houses. From the numerous examples given, it is hard to decide which is the most shocking. That concerning Turk's Head Yard, however, must be high on the list. Situated on the south side of Church Street, it formed a

> long irregular alley, rather narrow, paved and without efficient drains. Here are several filthy corners, and a very large cesspit, said to be the largest in the town, receiving the contents of six privies. Close by is a large slaughter-house in a dirty condition and giving out a most offensive smell. Mahommed's lodging house, in a dirty crowded condition, is in this yard.[22]

Such appalling health hazards were by no means confined to Turk's Head Court; nor do they complete the range of Preston's sanitary deficiences. To it can be added several manure deposits, composed of the ubiquitous night soil and street sweepings; that in Saul Street could accommodate a staggering 2,000 tons. There were also rough and irregular cobbled streets which retained pools of stagnant water and were difficult to clean. Even more disgusting were some of the town's 17 burial grounds, those belonging to the churches of St Peter and St Paul receiving particular opprobrium because of the obnoxious smells they generated. These owed much to the practice of burying paupers in large, open pits, which were only gradually covered with earth as layers of coffins were completed.[23]

The squalid conditions reported by Clay and Clark reflect only too clearly the shortcomings of Preston's sewerage system and water supply. Clark points out that only about one quarter of the total street length was drained by covered sewers. Altogether, four main sewers were provided, running across the town in an east-west direction and exiting into the lower reaches of the Ribble, partly along open ditches.[24] According to a report published in 1857, most were in an unsatisfactory condition, deficiencies including a lack of mortar in the brickwork, allowing seepage; too large a sectional area, which encouraged deposition of sewage; and insufficient depth, so that cellars could not always drain into them.[25]

As to water supply, inadequacies are reported in both availability and quality. Regarding the former, Clark points out that as many as 3,000 of the town's 8,000 houses were not connected to the mains. Accordingly, households commonly relied on the contents of rainwater butts.[26] Moreover, whilst the mains water pressure may have been sufficient to jet water over three-storeyed houses in the lowest parts of the town, it was not strong enough everywhere to dispense with pumps in case of fire. This was because the service reservoir at Ribbleton stood only 30 ft. above the highest part of the town. There was also concern that the water company had provided too few fire-plugs in their mains, so that 'large masses of valuable and highly inflammable property' remained at risk.[27]

Concerning water quality, the general complaint was made that the water company did not operate a filtration system, relying instead on impurities in the water being naturally deposited. In fact, some remarkably pure spring and stream water fed into the company's reservoirs; that from Cowley Brook was amongst the purest ever analysed in England or abroad. Yet impurities from surface rain, field drains and floods contaminated the service reservoir, water samples taken from it registering high levels of both saline and organic matter.[28]

Faced with such basic shortcomings in sewerage and water supply, it is hardly surprising that public health issues were of great concern to contemporaries. All too many of them led their daily lives in drab, squalid and smelly surroundings, which posed considerable risks to health. Indeed, if figures calculated by Clay are to be believed, early Victorian Preston was a particularly dangerous place to live. Taking the mean of a six-year period during the 1840s, he found the rate of mortality in the town to be very nearly three per cent, half as much again as the rate that was usual elsewhere in the country. Put another way, some 2,800 deaths occurred in Preston during the six-year period from causes which were 'susceptible of great control'.[29] Such dreadful statistics lend strong support to the claim that Preston's mortality levels were not exceeded by those in any other town in the country.[30]

Appalling though these figures are, they do not reveal the full tragedy of the situation, for they disguise the horrific levels of Preston's child mortality. One calculation suggests that almost half the town's children died before they reached five years of age.[31] All too often, local families suffered the loss of more than one child, as parish register entries and gravestone inscriptions so movingly demonstrate.

Such a high level of unnecessary deaths is a powerful reminder that early Victorian Preston was by no means the idyllic place that some contemporaries implied. It is true that parts of the town were worthy of appreciative comment, especially the stylish developments of high quality housing in and around Winckley Square, and there was much to commend in the architectural innovation brought to the town by buildings in the new Gothic-revival style. Yet there were many parts of the town that were singularly drear and unwholesome, not only providing the most disgusting living conditions, but also posing severe threats to public health. At the root of the problem lay the inadequacy of the town's sanitation provision, improvement to which had not kept pace with the town's expansion. Indeed, in the absence of a local sanitary authority to co-ordinate reform, it had no hope of so doing. Unfortunately this was a situation all too familiar in early Victorian towns.

References

1. G. Head, *A Home Tour through the Manufacturing Districts of England* (1968 reprint of 1836 edition), pp.413-14.
2. C. Hardwick, *History of the Borough of Preston* (1857), pp.451-53.
3. Mannex & Co., *The History ... of the Borough of Preston* (1851), p.46.
4. Ibid., pp.42-43.
5. Hardwick, *op. cit.*, p.537.
6. Mannex, *op. cit.*, p.42.
7. E. Butterworth, *A Statistical Sketch of the County Palatine of Lancaster* (1841), p.110.
8. J. Whittle, *History of the Borough of Preston* (1857), Vol. 1, p.118.
9. Mannex, *op. cit.*, p.44.

10. Whittle, *op. cit.*, Vol. 2, p.158.
11. Butterworth, *op. cit.*, p.111.
12. Whittle, *op. cit.*, Vol. 2, p.100.
13. I. Slater, *Commercial Directory and Topography of the County of Lancaster* (1851), p.426.
14. J. Whittle, *The Commercial Directory of Preston* (1841), p.8.
15. Mannex, *op. cit.*, pp.47-48.
16. Whittle, *op. cit.*, Vol. 2, p.101. A newspaper report reveals that the park was intended as a 100-acre cattle-grazing area, formed from the 240 acres of common land that comprised Preston Moor (*Preston Chronicle*, 14 September 1833). That the remaining land was to be sold or let allows a different interpretation to be placed on the actions of the Corporation. I am indebted to Nigel Morgan for drawing this to my attention.
17. Ibid., p.99.
18. J. Clay, *Report on the Sanitary Condition of the Borough of Preston* (1844), p.180.
19. Ibid., pp.194-95.
20. Ibid., pp.181-82.
21. They were located in Gilbert Street and Sergeant Street, near the junction of London Road and New Hall Lane (G. T. Clark, *Report to the General Board of Health ... on Preston* (1849), p.13).
22. Ibid., p.12.
23. Ibid., pp.28-29.
24. Ibid., pp.17-18.
25. *Report on the Sewerage of the Borough of Preston* (1857), p.1.
26. Clark, *op. cit.*, p.20.
27. *Reports on the Supply of Water to the Town of Preston* (1852), p.13.
28. Ibid., p.26.
29. Clay, *op. cit.*, p.166.
30. M. Anderson, *Family Structure in Nineteenth Century Lancashire* (1971), p.34.
31. Ibid., p.34.

32. The type of development to which Sir George Head refers included Avenham House, situated at the end of Avenham Walks. It was an unusual structure, with angled cornices and a projecting frontage supported by columns. The photograph was taken in the early 1860s.

33. This engraving, made in 1855, shows one view that could be obtained from Avenham Walks. The southern extremity of the town can be seen, including houses in Ribblesdale Place.

34. A classical-revival building, the Institute has a three-bay façade, the pediment above the entrance being supported by pilasters and a pair of fluted Corinthian columns. Wide steps with a curved balustrade lead to the doorway, at either side of which are deep, three-light windows. This photograph probably dates from the early 1900s.

35. Art classes formed an important part of the Institute's activities, the students in this photograph being at work around a century ago.

36. As the first of the engravings makes clear, Avenham Walks was still a favourite meeting place for polite society in the 1850s. By this time the Walks had been extended, steps at the end giving access to grassed terraces. These eventually became part of Avenham Park.

37. The visual appeal of Winckley Square owes much to the undulating parkland around which the buildings are grouped, as the 1850s engraving demonstrates. Most houses in the square were of a restrained classical style, those shown in the photographs, taken in the 1860s, being amongst the more visually impressive. The one above is of three-storeyed dwellings on the west side and the other of the house opposite, owned by William Ainsworth, a cotton mill owner. The square provided homes for Preston's leading citizens until the inter-war years, giving a powerful incentive for them to develop town-centre amenities. (See M. Savage, *The Dynamics of Working-Class Politics*, 1987, pp.113-15.)

38. Unfortunately the buildings in these engravings from the mid-1850s no longer stand. In the top left illustration, the block to the left comprised the Literary and Philosophical Institution and the Winckley Club. The former is identified by its two square towers, between which is a large, arched window. The latter adjoins the Institution to the left, being distinguished by a single square tower and oriel window. The photograph, taken in the 1930s, shows the position of the buildings in relation to the square. The remaining illustration is of the Grammar School in Cross Street, the most prominent characteristic of which was a pair of tall octagonal towers, surmounted by pointed domes.

39. The central and end blocks of Stephenson Terrace project slightly and are three storeys high. Unusually for houses in Preston, stone was preferred to brick. Altogether, 24 dwellings were built, each with a porch supported by undecorated columns.

40.   Again, as the engraving reveals, the Corn Exchange was a classical-style building, having a pediment and domed clock tower. The map extract (from the five feet to the mile O.S. survey of the 1840s) makes it clear that the building was used as a market for dairy produce and meat, as well as for corn.

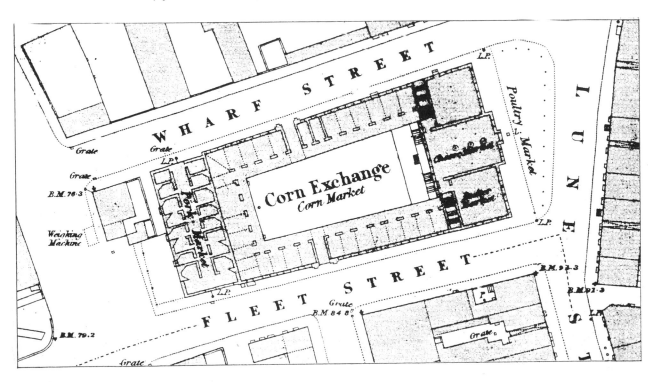

41. Public meetings were also held at the Exchange; that shown in the above photograph was probably taken to commemorate the golden jubilee of teetotalism, a movement with which Preston is particularly associated. The exterior photograph shows the appearance of the building after it was converted to a public hall in 1882. Most of the building was demolished in 1991 to make way for road improvements, and only the restored front block survives.

42. Built of Longridge stone, Fulwood Barracks was opened in 1848 and cost the not insubstantial sum of £137,921. Its outer gateway, shown in the above engraving, has been demolished, but the chapel, with its arched windows, cupola and pedimented central bays, has survived.

43. The chapel frontage, shown here in 1905, overlooks one of the parade grounds, around which are grouped two-storeyed living quarters. The photograph of the two women and child was taken outside the married soldiers' quarters *c*.1920.

44. The fortress-like style of the former governor's house may seem curious, since the prison, of which it forms part, aims to confine people rather than to repel them. Nevertheless, the building adds interesting variety to the town's architecture, though it is unfortunately screened from view by a line of trees. The interior photograph, taken in the 1930s, reveals the familiar design for a Victorian prison, with rows of cells, one above the other, accessed by open-tread stairways and narrow landings.

45. St Peter's church is one of two Preston churches financed largely by parliamentary grants made available through the Church Building Commission. The other, also shown here, is St Paul's. The aim was to lessen the threat of social unrest by ensuring that rapidly-growing populations in urban areas had sufficient places of worship. The commissioners preferred churches to be in the Gothic style on grounds of cheapness. (See K. Clark, *The Gothic Revival*, 1962, pp.94-99.)

46. The nearer bridge was built in 1846 to take the East Lancashire line over the Ribble. It originally comprised three segmented arches constructed from iron, supported by two brick and stone piers and by a semicircular stone arch at each side. The more distant was erected in 1838 for the North Union Railway. It is composed of impressively large blocks of rusticated stone, as the photograph, taken in the 1860s, shows.

47.   The Shaw illustration of the 1880s certainly gives the impression of a busy station. The narrow frontage of the ticket office building lessens the impact of its classical-style features, architectural detail in any case being confined to the upper storeys. More striking are the wide, shallow-arched platform canopies, supported by rows of cast-iron columns.

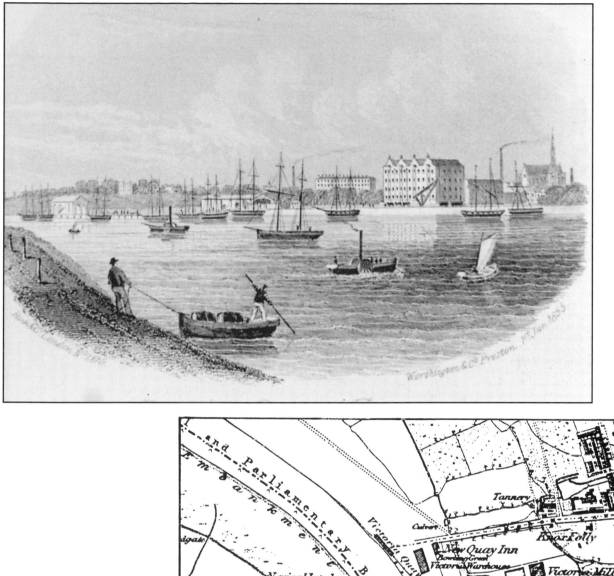

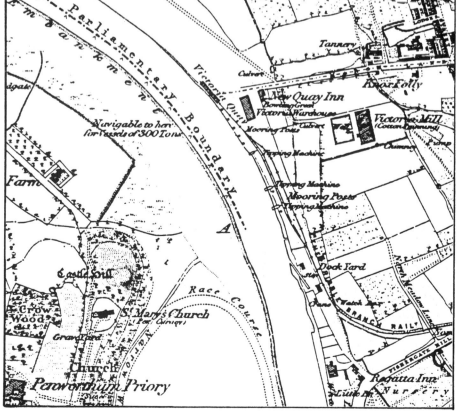

48. The new bonded warehouse, a substantial five-storeyed structure with front gables, is shown on both the 1840s O.S. map and the 1850s engraving. By this time, the quayside was linked to the rail network, along which coal would have been brought to discharge into ships, probably making use of the tipping machines.

49. The land for Moor Park was enclosed in 1834 from the town's common land. Soon afterwards Moor Park Avenue, a tree-lined promenade some three-quarters of a mile long, was constructed, with lodges at either end. These were built in the fashionable Gothic style, that shown being at the west end. A serpentine lake was also provided and was graced by swans. The photographs date from the early 20th century.

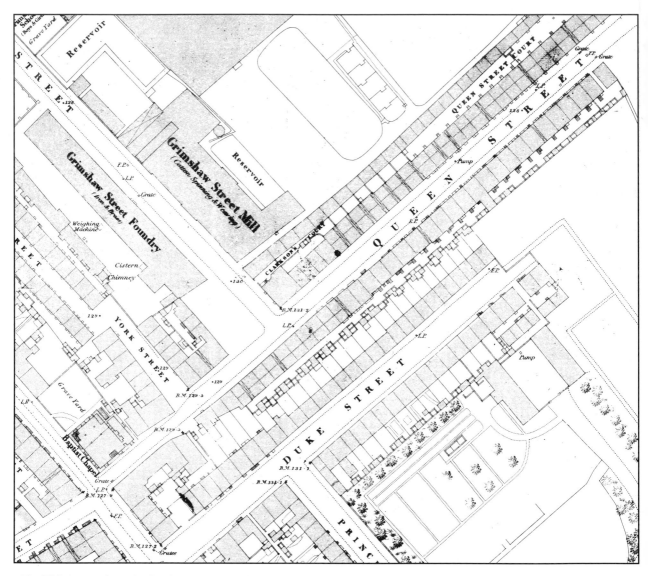

50.   This extract from the five feet to the mile O.S. map of the 1840s confirms the closeness of the privies to the houses. Here, in fact, was a long and narrow back yard, which, if the tenants of all the back-to-back dwellings in the row are included, was shared by no fewer than 32 households.

51. The health hazards of such arrangements are not difficult to imagine, nor are the foul odours that would have prevailed.

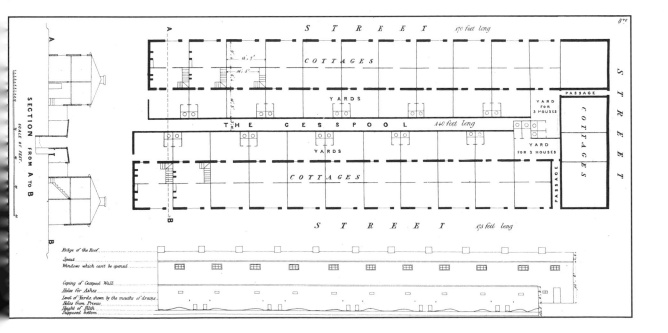

52.   Other examples of the type of insanitary housing found in Preston at this time include the cellar dwellings at Kirkham Street (off Fylde Road) and the two-up, two-down cottages in Cotton Court (off Church Street). Because they have their own entrances and a limited window area, the former were probably purpose-built dwellings rather than conversions from former hand weavers' cottages. The latter illustrate the process by which burgage plots were infilled. As was common in Preston the pavements were cobbled, the raw material, no doubt, being obtained from the Ribble. Setts were preferred for the road. Both photographs were probably taken in the 1930s.

3. Victorian and Edwardian Developments

Comparison of the 1846 and 1913 Ordnance Survey maps of Preston (front and back endpapers) reveals the tremendous extent to which the town grew during Victorian and Edwardian times. At the start of Victoria's reign, a walk from the Market Square to any part of the built-up area could be comfortably undertaken within 10 minutes; by the Edwardian years, the time taken would generally have doubled.

One of the most striking features of this growth is the emergence of the town's first residential suburbs. Located at Fulwood, about a mile and a half to the north of the town centre, and at Ashton, a similar distance to the north-west, the suburbs offered higher standards of accommodation at the upper end of the housing market [53]. No longer were the better-off confined to town-centre terraces, however elegant and substantial these may have been. Now they could live in rural surroundings, where detached and semi-detached dwellings set in generously-sized plots gave far greater privacy, as well as a more wholesome and healthy environment [54 & 55]. There was, it is true, the inconvenience of living at a distance from town-centre facilities, but many residents could afford to provide their own means of transport, or could use the horse-drawn buses and later the trams, which linked both Ashton and Fulwood with the town centre [56].[1] Even allowing for the slowness of horse-drawn vehicles and for the congestion in town-centre streets, the journey to and from the suburbs could scarcely have been regarded as time-consuming or arduous.

The low-density housing of the suburbs contrasted sharply with the type of development taking place more generally in Preston. For the most part, this comprised closely-packed, grid-iron terraces spreading out from the town centre and clustering around the ever-growing number of textile mills [57]. Such development was concentrated on the northern and eastern fringes. On the south side, urban spread was checked by the Ribble flood plain and by the creation of Miller Park and Avenham Park during the early 1860s [58 & 59].[2] To the west, barriers were provided by Ashton Park (property of the Pedders) and the docks.[3]

Characteristically, Preston's Victorian terraces were built without a back street or passage, as the extract from the 1913 O.S. map reveals [60]. Household waste, including excreta, had to be carried through narrow passages known locally as lobbies, one of which was shared between each pair of houses [61]. In some late Victorian developments, back passages were provided between terraces, as the map extract shows, and these were wide enough to allow access for a horse and cart [62]. The advantage of such passages was not only that the unpleasantness associated with refuse disposal, principally the spillages and smells, could be kept away from the house, but also that the distance refuse had to be carried was greatly reduced. The disadvantage was that more land was required, a point that was not lost on builders and landowners in their opposition to back street provision.[4]

The general absence of back streets would have been less serious if Preston's Victorian terraces had been fitted with water closets, but few were. During the late 19th century, Preston's Medical Officer of Health, whose post was belatedly established under the provisions of the 1872 Public Health Act, often commented on this issue.[5] It was not until 1909, when the town's death rate was at last showing a marked decline, that he could report an almost complete conversion to a water closet system.[6]

The universal adoption of water closets depended upon the provision of an adequate sewerage system. This was not achieved until the early 1890s, when intercepting sewers were built to channel the sewage to a processing works at Freckleton, several miles down-river from the town.[7]

Significant progress was also made with regard to other aspects of public health. In 1853, the town's first cemetery was opened at Ribbleton, allowing church graveyards to be closed [63].[8] Improvements were also made to the water supply, including the abandonment of the low-level service reservoir at Ribbleton, thereby solving the problem of inadequate water pressure.[9] Yet the impact of these advances was diminished by the continuing inadequacies of house sanitation, which, in large measure, were responsible for Preston's stubbornly high death rate. Between 1880 and 1900, the town had the unenviable distinction of achieving the highest annual levels of infant mortality within large towns on no fewer than 15 occasions.[10]

As map evidence reveals, many of the mills around which Preston's industrial housing was built were sited alongside major lines of communication. This is clearly seen on the west side of the town, through which the canal and mainline railway both passed. It is also evident in the Deepdale area, to the east, where the Longridge railway terminated. How frequently Preston's textile mills linked directly with canal or railway is uncertain. Proximity to a canal wharf or railway siding would have brought useful economies, however, not least in transport costs. Nor should it be overlooked that mill builders often used sites alongside main roads, especially on the east side of town. These sites were beyond the central areas, so building land would have been relatively cheap.

The siting of Preston's other factory settlements is less easy to explain, though it is noticeable that a considerable number were situated in two tributary valleys of the Ribble. One, the Moor Brook valley (to the north of the town centre) had already acquired several cotton mills, though little housing, by the mid-1840s. The other, Swill Brook, situated on the south-east fringes of the town, developed rather later, though both had become densely populated industrial zones by the end of the century. Availability of water for steam raising may have influenced the choice of these valleys for mill building. Also, high natural humidity in valley floors would have proved especially useful in weaving cotton [64].[11]

As was generally the case, the design of Preston's cotton mills changed markedly during the Victorian and Edwardian years. At mid-century, the multi-storey spinning blocks tended to be plain and functional, their weight being taken mainly by a framework of cast-iron columns, and wooden beams. By the end of the century, steel-framed spinning blocks with cast-iron columns, concrete floors and arched brick ceilings became usual. Full opportunity was taken to embellish these mills, that at Tulketh showing regular courses of yellow brick amongst its predominantly red-brick courses [65].[12]

These later cotton mills added appreciably to Preston's architectural interest, a point which may not have appealed readily to those who laboured such long hours in them. Indeed, the town's industrial communities were by no means devoid of stylish buildings, especially churches and chapels. Amongst them St Walburge's, with its 300-ft. steeple, the third highest in the country, is outstanding. As one leading authority has observed, it is a steeple 'one does not forget, of white stone whereas the rest is brown,and excessively slender, almost ghost-like' [66].[13]

St Walburge's was erected during the early 1850s (the tower and spire being added during the following decade) at a time when church builders had begun to imitate, with great accuracy, the decorated styles of architecture which were fashionable during the late 13th and early 14th centuries.[14] Some of the finest examples in Preston are to be found at the parish church of St John the Divine, in Church Street, rebuilt in the mid-1850s, and on the west front of St Thomas and English Martyrs, erected beside Garstang Road in 1863-7 [67].

Fortunately this change in fashion did not constrain church architects too closely, nor too long, and those responsible for designing Preston's Victorian churches were fully prepared to realise their own preferences, or those of their clients. Some persevered with Gothic revivalism, but did not always adopt the decorated styles. For instance, an Early English style was chosen for St Luke's church and a mixture of decorated and Early English for St Joseph's [68]. Others remained loyal to the classical tradition, at least in part, and were quite ready to indulge their own flights of fancy. Particularly striking examples are St Wilfrid's church in Chapel Street [69], St Augustine's church at Frenchwood, and Fishergate Baptist church [70 & 71]. Classical styles were also favoured for Nonconformist chapels, Preston's finest examples being the former Moor Park Methodist in Garstang Road and the Central Methodist in Lune Street [72], both with striking entrances.

The battle of the revivalist styles is less evident in the development of Preston's Victorian and Edwardian public buildings. Most of the major ones are clustered around the old market square in the centre of town [73] and are mainly the product of redevelopment during the late 19th and early 20th centuries [74, 75 & 76]. They represent a triumphant victory for the classicists. The ideas they embody are seen at their most imposing in the case of the Harris Library and Museum [77 & 78] and at their most lavish in the Baroque decoration of Miller Arcade [79] and Sessions House [80]. The remaining buildings, comprising the post office [81 & 82], the former courthouse, and central police station, which dates partly from the late 1850s [83], and the Town Hall, a product of the 1930s [84], are more restrained in terms of architectural detail, but harmonise well and add scale and dignity to the square. Whether such comments can be applied with equal conviction to Crystal House, a modern high-rise block occupying the southern side of the square, is debatable. But this building has laboured under the disadvantage of replacing Preston's much-revered Victorian Town Hall, a bold expression of Gothic revivalism, which burned down in 1947 [85 to 88].

In terms of both scale and appearance, then, Preston was a substantially different place in the early 20th century than it had been half a century or so before. Yet it remained a town of marked contrasts. It is true that a good deal of environmental improvement took place, producing churches and public buildings of distinction, as well as houses, some of them for working-class people, that set new standards in hygiene, privacy and design. At the same time, however, most Prestonians continued to live in conditions which, though showing appreciable sanitary improvement by the late Victorian years, were still cramped, overcrowded and damp. Nor was air pollution adequately tackled. In such circumstances, it is arguable whether civic responsibility was as much to the fore as civic pride.

References

1. For details, see G. W. Heywood, 'The Tramways of Preston', *Tramway Review*, 9 (1971), pp.67-75.
2. For details, see A. Hewitson, *History of Preston* (1883), pp.319-26.
3. On Ashton Park, see C. Hardwick, *History of the Borough of Preston* (1857), pp.75-78.
4. N. Morgan, *An Introduction to the Social History of Housing in Preston*, n.d., pp.75-78.
5. Ibid., pp.70-72.
6. *Annual Report of the Medical Officer of Health* (1908), p.17.
7. P. Barrett & Co., *General and Commercial Directory of Preston and Fylde Districts* (1910), p.17.
8. Hardwick, *op. cit.*, pp.484-85.
9. J. Wilkinson, *Preston's Royal Infirmary* (1987), p.41.
10. Morgan, *op. cit.*, p.87.
11. The influence of humidity was much more important in cotton weaving than in cotton spinning. See D. A. Farnie, *The English Cotton Industry and the World Market, 1815-1896* (1979), p.48.
12. Details of changes in textile mill design can be found in O. Ashmore, *The Industrial Archaeology of Lancashire* (1969), pp.47-52.
13. N. Pevsner, *The Buildings of England: North Lancashire* (1969), p.200.
14. Ibid., pp.31-32.

53. The map extracts are from the 25 inches to the mile O.S. map of 1913. They suggest that Fulwood was the more exclusive of the two suburbs, being more clearly separated from industry and working-class terraces, and bordering Moor Park to the south.

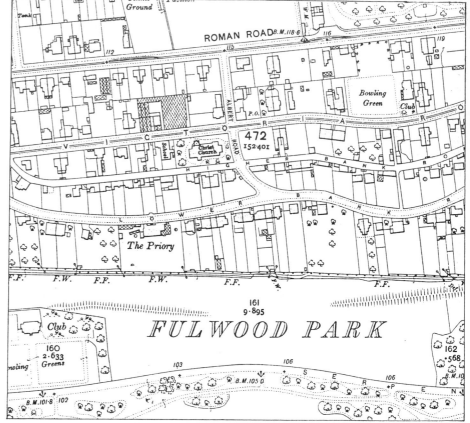

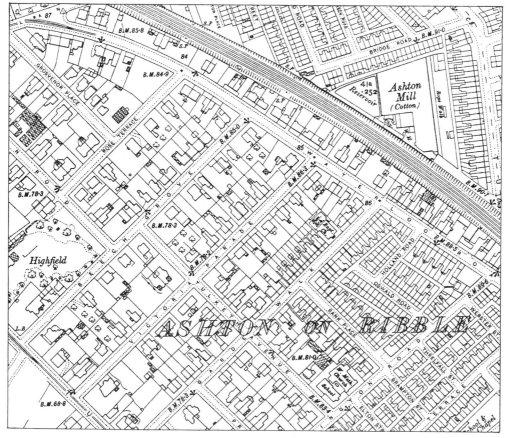

54. These postcard illustrations, probably dating from the early 20th century, give views along Watling Street Road, Fulwood. The houses are substantial, some with second-floor gable windows, indicating the provision of attic rooms for resident servants.

55. Churches were amongst the early public facilities provided at Fulwood, most notably the Wesleyan church and the Anglican Christ Church. Both have octagonal towers set on a square base, the Wesleyan church, built in brick and stone, being highly ornate. The Christ Church photograph, taken in the early 1860s, shows women who appear to be dressed in crinolines.

56. These photographs depict various types of public transport that serviced the Fulwood suburb. The horse-drawn tram dates from the mid-Victorian era, the electric tram from the early 20th century, and the motor bus from the 1920s. (For details of the general development of Fulwood, see Carole Knight, *Step back in Time: A History of Fulwood*, 1986.)

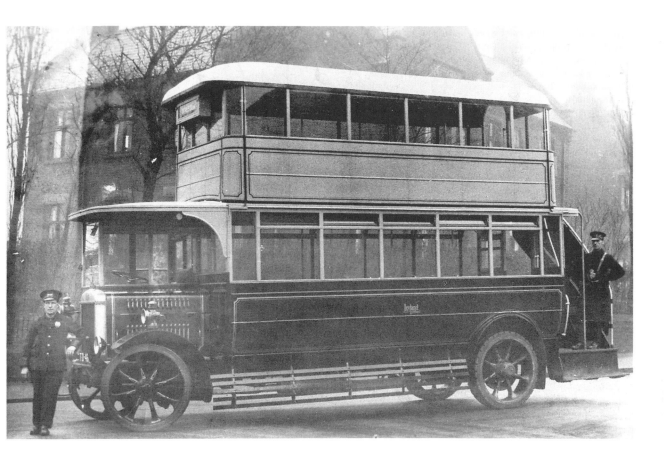

57. Part of Preston's Victorian development, though, comprised further construction of middle-class houses for those who, along with the Winckley Square élite, still preferred the convenience of living near to the town centre. The examples shown, situated along the south side of Fishergate Hill, were given fashionable bay windows and were built three storeys high. The photograph dates from *c*.1912.

58. The Miller Park photographs probably date from the early 20th century. One shows the fanciful architecture of the former *Park Hotel*, distinguished by ornate chimney-stacks, front gables and a tall, square tower with pyramid roof, giving magnificent views over the surrounding countryside. The other records a group of young girls, complete with wide-brimmed hats and doll's conveyance.

59.   A major attraction at Avenham Park was the bandstand, Sunday afternoon concerts proving popular with family groups. Sufficient space was available to permit large public gatherings, one of which was encouraged by children singing to commemorate the jubilee of George V in 1935.

60.   Numerous examples of houses without back streets can be seen to the north of Fishwick Parade.

61. Lobby doorways were often less ornate than the doorways at either side, but in more stylish houses they sometimes form an integral part of the façade architecture. Both approaches can be viewed as an attempt to disguise the existence of the lobby. The above example of the former type was photographed in Bedford Street during the mid-1960s, whilst that below can be seen in East Cliffe Road. The example of the latter type is in Waltons Parade.

62. Back streets had appeared in Preston before the late Victorian years, but were not necessarily wide enough to take a horse and cart. The example shown is between Hall Place and Butler Street. The frontages of back-street houses are characterised by an absence of lobby doors and frequently by considerable ornamentation, a reflection of the late period at which they were built. Those at Bank Street, Ashton, were given bay windows and front gardens. The photograph probably dates from c.1900.

63.   The top postcard records the ornate cemetery gates and lodges, built in Gothic style. Particularly striking are the Tudor-style chimney-stacks. The other illustration depicts the Anglican chapel at the cemetery. Both postcards date from the early 20th century.

64. Power weaving sheds were usually single-storey structures with saw-tooth roofs, the glazed sections of which faced north. They were angled steeply enough to prevent the sun's rays shining directly into the shed, even at midsummer. The photograph of this weaving shed, which was part of Brookfield Mill, shows its low-lying position in Moor Brook Valley.

65. The first of Preston's steel-framed mills was Centenary, built in 1895 by the Horrocks concern. Situated in New Hall Lane, it is a four-storeyed structure, with pronounced corner towers and shallow-arched windows. The high ratio of window to wall area in both these mills ensures good natural lighting inside. The photograph dates from the early 1900s.

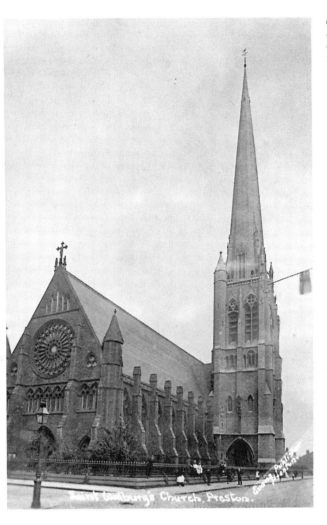

66. The photograph shows the west end of St Walburge's church with its prominent rose window. Inside, as the engraving reveals, the church is without aisles and has a remarkable hammerbeam roof, very steeply pitched.

Interior of St Walburgh's Church, Preston

St Walburgh's Church & Talbot School, Preston

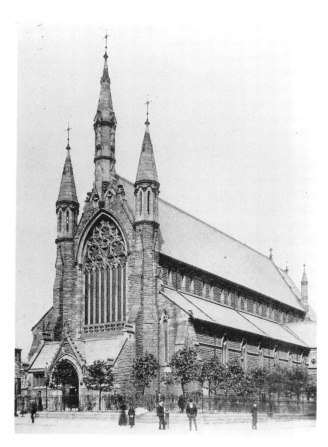

67. The decorated style was considered to be Gothic architecture at its most complete. Window tracery provides its most prominent characteristic. This can be geometrical, which consists principally of small, intersecting arcs (foils) terminating in cusps (points). Those at St Thomas' and English Martyrs' church have four-foil (quatrefoil) and multi-foil decoration inside circles. Later decorated styles incorporate flowing tracery, the patterns being freer, as the examples from the parish church demonstrate. One has quatrefoil decoration but with the top and bottom foils drawn into points, giving ogee arches. The other has mouchette (curved dagger) decoration, in this case with one handle serving two blades. The photograph of St Thomas' and English Martyrs' church dates from 1902.

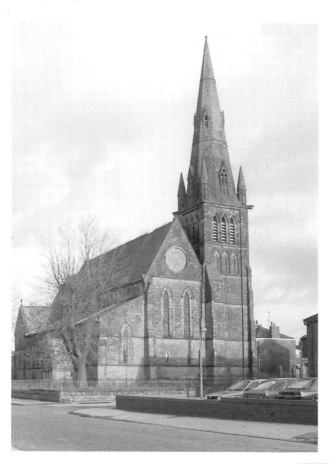

68. Lancet windows characterise St Luke's church in Fletcher Road, opened in 1859, and St Joseph's in Skeffington Road, dating from 1874. At St Joseph's, however, there is also geometrical tracery.

69. The above illustration is of St Wilfred's church before it was refurbished *c*.1880. Brick-built, it had pronounced quoins (corner stones) with arcading in the side wall rising high above the pedimented windows. The modern photograph shows the elaborate decoration added, extensive use being made of smooth, Accrington brick and brown terracotta.

70. St Augustine's church was opened in 1840, its principal external feature being a four-columned portico with Ionic capitals and pediment. Late-Victorian alterations raised the height of the church, and corner towers with cupolas were added.

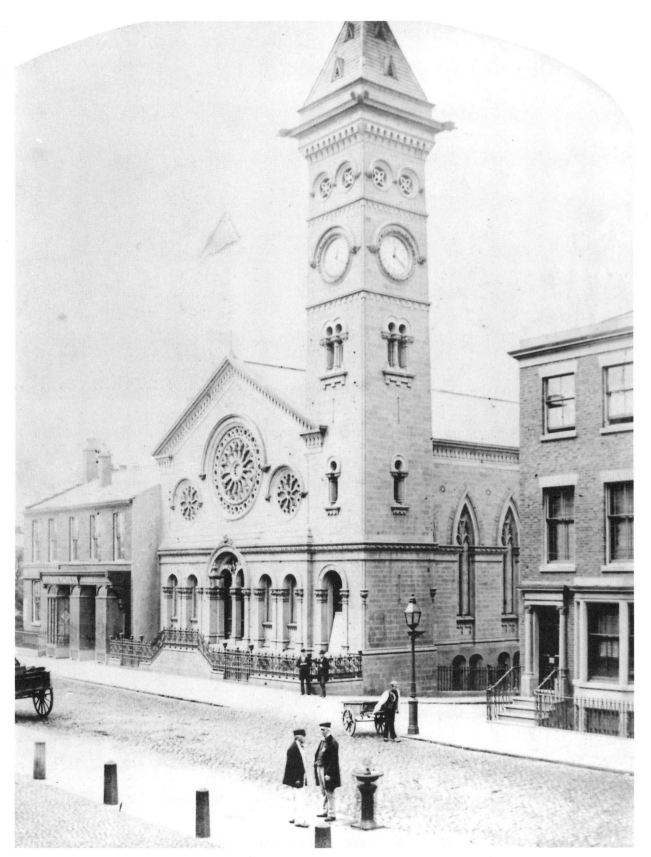

71. Fishergate Baptist church, dating from the late 1850s, is highly individualistic, mainly inspired by Norman architecture, but with Gothic detail, including pointed side windows. The photograph dates from the early 1860s.

5

72. Moor Park Methodist church was erected in 1861 and has a huge, semicircular porch supported by Ionic columns. It was still in use during the mid-1960s when this photograph was taken. The Central Methodist chapel dates from 1817. It was altered in the early 1860s, however, when the massive entrance with its paired columns and pediment were added. Sadly, the gate posts and wrought-iron gates have been removed. This photograph was taken in 1937.

73. The most notable public buildings situated beyond the town centre are the former union workhouse at Watling Street Road, Fulwood, and County Hall in Fishergate. The workhouse, erected during the late 1860s, has a classical-style façade which is impressive in both scale and appearance. It could accommodate 1,500 paupers. In common with other Victorian workhouses, this was an expensive building. Loan charges against it, which ratepayers had to meet, stood at a sizeable £90,000 in 1870. (For details, see E. Midwinter, *Social Administration in Lancashire, 1830-60*, 1969, pp.56-57.)

County Hall comprises an extensive range of buildings, the earliest part of which, shown in the illustration, was opened in 1882. A strong Tudor influence is evident, with mullioned and transomed windows, decorated gables and tall, ornamented chimney stacks.

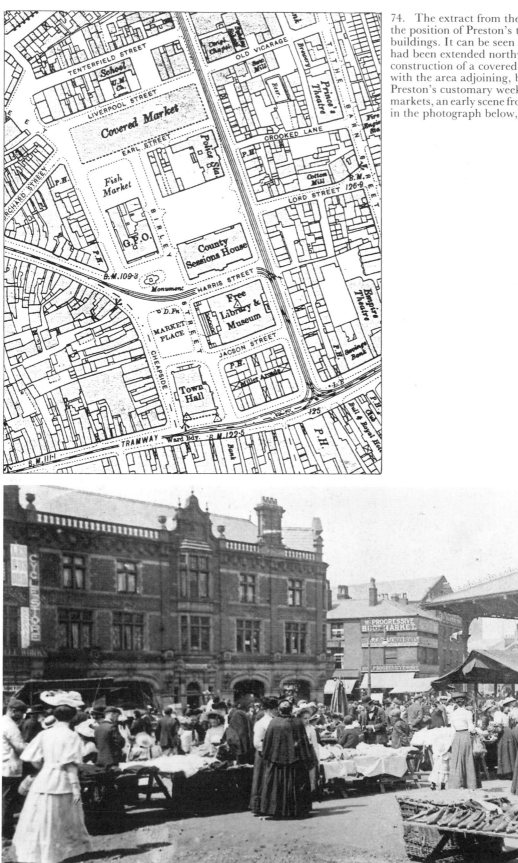

74. The extract from the 1913 O.S. map gives the position of Preston's town-centre public buildings. It can be seen that the development had been extended northwards by the construction of a covered market. This, along with the area adjoining, became the venue for Preston's customary weekday and Saturday markets, an early scene from which can be seen in the photograph below, taken c.1906.

75. Other events which took place in the covered market included cheese fairs, which aroused appreciable interest. The photograph may date from the inter-war years.

76. The Market Place continued to be used for its traditional function, as this 1908 photograph confirms. Curiously, only one stallholder is trading.

77. Financed from the will of E. R. Harris, the Harris Library, Museum and Art Gallery was completed in 1891, and is shown here in a photograph taken in the same year. It rests on an elevated base of rusticated stone, with a three-storey frontage and massive lantern tower rising from its centre. The frontage is dominated by a row of six Ionic columns, fluted and carrying a pediment with sculptures. Amongst the property demolished to make way for the new building was the distinctive row of shops in the Old Shambles, traditionally the centre of the butchers' trade.

78. The readers shown in the first interior photograph, taken *c*.1900, are sitting at separate tables according to gender. They have retained their outer garments. The other interior photograph, taken in 1935, is of the newly opened children's library.

MILLER ARCADE
PRESTON

BIRCH

TEEDEE
SERIES

79. Miller arcade, opened in 1901, is square in plan,
with external walls in brick and terracotta. Features
include built-in corner turrets with first-floor balconies
and an elaborate frieze between first- and second-floor
levels. The photograph depicts it in the early 20th
century. From inside, the glazed, semicircular roof
with cast-iron ribs can be viewed, along with rich wall
decorations of flowers, fruits and leaves. (For further
details see Margaret McKeith, *Shopping Arcades*, 1986,
pp.121-22.)

PRESTON, NEW SESSIONS HOUSE.

E.T.W.D.

80. Sessions House (1901-3) has a four-tiered, central tower, which rises to a height of 170 ft. and is crowned by a pinnacle. Each tier is smaller than the one beneath and columns of varying arrangement form a key feature. The ground-floor walls are of rusticated stone, with ashlar above. Pairs of Ionic columns flank the outer and central bays. The photograph would have been taken soon after the building was completed.

81. Built in 1903, the post office has gabled bays at each end. Window design varies at each floor level, culminating in a row of round-arched dormers. The photograph showing a rather formal and cheerless interior was taken in 1932.

82. In 1926 the present cenotaph, situated at the front of the post office was unveiled, replacing the ealier Boer War
memorial.

83. The 1901 extension to the courthouse and former police station closely imitates the style of the original building (which dates from the late 1850s) adding a three-storeyed tower and southern wing.

84. The Town Hall is unusual in that its architectural detail is almost the same on both front and rear walls. As the 1933 photograph reveals, it is rusticated at ground-floor level. This feature is continued at the edges of the three end bays which, at each side of the façade, stand proud below top-storey level. The opening ceremony in 1933 provided a major civic occasion, whilst the interior of the new building attracted a good deal of public interest, not least from schoolchildren.

85. The mid-Victorian engraving shows the redesigned south side of the Market Square, graced by Sir George Gilbert Scott's Town Hall. Opened in 1867, it was the one major Gothic-style building to penetrate the centre of Preston. The early photograph of the building shows the Fishergate frontage.

20266. TOWN HALL, PRESTON. Foulton.

86. The photograph of the Town Hall vestibule demonstrates the meticulous attention paid to architectural detail, with patterned tiling, polished granite pillars, decorated arches and, to add the finishing touch, sculptures on pedestals. Tragically, the building was badly damaged by fire in 1947 and the remains demolished in 1962.

87. That Scott's Town Hall is held in such affection may be partly explained by the association it had with major landmarks in Preston's history. This view shows the return of First World War soldiers.

88. This photograph depicts the reception held for the Preston North End football team after its F.A. cup final victory in 1938.

Conclusion

Preston's recorded history occupies a time-span of around a thousand years. Yet it is only within the last two hundred or so years that the town has achieved anything more than regional significance. Indeed, as late as 1801 it ranked merely thirtieth amongst English provincial towns in terms of population size. Sixty years later, following a remarkable sevenfold increase in population, its position had risen to an impressive thirteenth.[1]

The emergence of Preston as a leading town is closely associated with the development of textile production, especially the growth of a factory-based cotton industry during the Victorian era. The requirements of this trade for additional industrial premises and housing, along with the wealth it generated, profoundly altered the size of the town and the character of its built environment. In fact, as far as some contemporaries were concerned, these changes were so momentous that ambitions of attaining city status could be seriously entertained.

Viewed in long-term perspective, however, the dominance of the cotton industry in Preston was comparatively short-lived. Its decline after World War One was relentless, albeit protracted. Between the outbreaks of the First and Second World Wars, around thirty of the town's cotton mills closed,[2] and by 1948, the textile trades as a whole, which then included rayon manufacture, comprised only around 15 per cent of the town's labour force.[3] As mill closures continued unabated during the immediate post-war decades, Preston ceased to be a cotton town of any significance. In common with so many towns that grew to prominence on the basis of manufacturing activity, it became primarily a centre for service industries.

Inevitably, the change from a manufacturing to a service economy has had a marked impact on Preston's built environment. This is at its most obvious in terms of townscape, with the textile mill chimney being replaced by the high-rise office block. But it can also be seen in the development of retail superstores, mainly located in new shopping centres on the town outskirts; the expansion of educational facilities, especially for higher-level work; and the provision of industrial estates, mainly on the north-east outskirts of town, where both service sector and manufacturing activities are accommodated.

Accompanying these changes have been improvements to the town's road network, especially to the south, where a fourth road bridge has been built across the Ribble. There has also been substantial housing development beyond the town centre, most notably at Ingol to the north-west and Penwortham to the south-west. Thus, both the town's employment and housing has become more widely dispersed, relieving pressure on town-centre facilities and taking advantage of the marketing opportunities arising from growing car ownership.

Yet the impact of such changes should not be exaggerated. Much remains of the Preston that developed during the cotton textile era, both in the town centre and on the outskirts. With regard to the former, the major public buildings around the old market-place provide the most striking examples. Viewed from the front, their impact is somewhat muted by Crystal House and the Guild Hall, but, thankfully, only glimpses can be obtained of the high-rise blocks beyond. Additionally, stylish Victorian bank and shop façades can still be found in some quantity, especially along Fishergate and some of its side streets. Indeed, to look along Fishergate, especially from the western end, is to gain the impression of a street which, despite piecemeal redevelopment, is still largely composed of Victorian and Edwardian buildings.

Away from the town centre, the Victorian era is well represented by former mill-workers' terraces. Many are in improvement areas, pointing to what might have been achieved on a larger scale, both in Preston and elsewhere, had policies of refurbishment been more enthusiastically adopted during earlier decades. Here, too, are a number of Victorian churches, some of them disused, and textile mills, most of them reused. The removal of the chimney stacks belonging to these mills has had the welcome effect of allowing the towers and steeples of the churches, which are by no means numerous, to achieve a much greater prominence as townscape features. Much survives, too, of the early middle-class suburbs at Fulwood and Ashton. These still adjoin parkland, though they are now engulfed by later development and, in consequence, no longer provide the degree of exclusiveness which those who built them strove to achieve.

To end by emphasising continuity rather than change is fitting in a publication appearing during a Guild year. Understandably, such an occasion focuses attention on tradition, giving opportunity to reflect on Preston's past achievements and to recognise that each generation has played its part, however small, in helping to create a major town. This recognition is important, because it forms the vital first step in appreciating the value of these achievements, not least with regard to the town's built environment. Without it, appropriate strategies for conservation and redevelopment are unlikely to be achieved, with past buildings being too readily dismissed as 'old-fashioned' or 'in bad taste'. Indeed, it is as instructive as it is fascinating to decide which amongst Preston's demolished buildings would now be regarded as visual assets to the town had this, or previous generations chosen to conserve them.

References
1. W. G. Hoskins, *Local History in England* (1959), p.178.
2. T. C. Dickinson, *Lancashire Under Steam* (1984), p.41.
3. *Development Plan for the County Borough of Preston* (1951), Table 14.

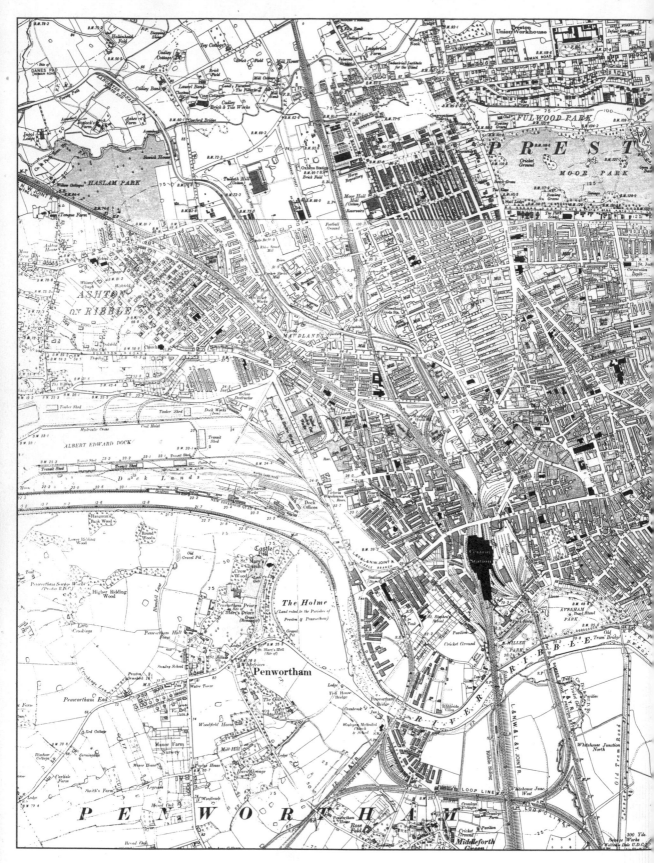

O.S. Map, 1913.